David, you're
Now you're a man. Here's your
guide to the future!

- Eric

Be Warned

A number of the entries in this book are highly dangerous and should only ever be approached with extreme caution. For example, while *Man Skills* suggests how best to jump from a speeding train or escape from a shark, these are to be used only as last resorts when all other hope has left the building. Only if you're a trained expert should you attempt any skill where your life is put in danger. The information contained in these pages is correct to the best of the author and publisher's knowledge and backed up by experts, but there are just too many variables to cover every situation. If you go out of your way to wrestle alligators, for example, based on the advice on page 145, you'll almost certainly get everything you deserve.

So, just to reiterate, we—the author, all experts involved, the publishers and everyone we know—disclaim any responsibility from any injury or death that may occur from following the guidance in this book. Equally, none of the skills here should be used to break any laws or infringe on the rights of any other person or persons.

Behave yourselves; be nice to each other and everything should be just fine.

Nick Harper

★ MAN ★

Skills

EVERYTHING MEN NEED (or Just Want) TO KNOW

by Nick Harper

SOURCEBOOKS HYSTERIA™
AN IMPRINT OF SOURCEBOOKS, INC.®
NAPERVILLE, ILLINOIS

Published by Sourcebooks Hysteria, an imprint of Sourcebooks, Inc.
P.O. Box 4410, Naperville, Illinois 60567-4410
(630) 961-3900
Fax: (630) 961-2168
www.sourcebooks.com

Originally published in Great Britain in 2006 by Michael O'Mara
Books Limited

Library of Congress Cataloging-in-Publication Data

Harper, Nick.
  Man skills : everything men need (or just want) to know / by Nick
Harper.
     p. cm.
  ISBN 978-1-4022-1052-5 (trade pbk.)
  1. Men--Life skills guides. 2. Men--Psychology. 3. Masculinity. I.
Title.

HQ1090.H374 2007
646.70081--dc22

                                          2007027188

Contents

Acknowledgments

Humble thanks, in no particular order, to Mark Pitt, Mike Glendinning, Phil and Jayne, Ben and Karen, Matt and Mel, Ian Quest, Dan Jones, Richard and Tanya, Simon Weeden, Ma and Pa Harper and Burdett, Lawrence and Fiona, Scott Murray, Dan Rookwood, Rob Smyth, Simon 'Dogs' Burdett and Muneni, Matt Pool, Boris, Toby Potter, Tom Goss, Chris and Claire, Michael Powell, all at MOM (particularly Chris and Lindsay), David Woodroffe, Al, Peaches, Mooro, and Ollie, who sorted it.

Most thanks of all to Sarah, for the many years of patience.

The Experts:
Champagne and Wine entries Bon Vivant Harry Putt (www.winefoodacademy.com)

Survive in Prison Peter Harper, Prison Officer, Buckley Hall Prison

Dive Like Tarzan Rob 'Frenchy' French, Playboy Lifeguard

Heimlich, CPR, Bleeding and Burns Joe Mulligan, Head of First Aid Services, Red Cross

Shake Hands Properly Thomas Blaikie, author of *Blaikie's Guide To Modern Manners* (Fourth Estate, 2005)

Deliver a Baby Virginia Howes, Independent Midwife (www.kentmidwiferypractice.co.uk)

All Car and Driving Skills Alan 'AJ' Jeffrey, Former Rally Driver and Technical Author

Catch a Fish with String Patrick McGlinchey, Survival Expert (www.backwoodssurvival.co.uk)

Pull Your Own Tooth 'No, Don't'–Dr Martin S. Spiller, Responsible Dentist

Hit the Hammer Thing Paul Jose of Fun Time Hire, Hammer Expert

Take a Punch Jezz Wilcox, Personal Trainer (www.thethirdspace.com)

Dance Moves Brent Ingleton, Club Moves Instructor (www.danceworks.net); mental tips: Jacqueline Butler, Dance Instructor

Jump from a Speeding Train Jon Epstein, Chuck Norris's stunt double

Mow the Lawn Mick Hunt, Head Groundsman, Lord's Cricket Club

Throw Like a Man Patrick Fallis, Cricket Coach (www.coachingcricketexcellence.co.uk)

Buy Flowers Samantha Bayton, Flowergram Ltd (www.flowergram.co.uk)

Mix a Cocktail Juha Kaskinen, Founder of London's Cocktail Academy (www.cocktailacademy.co.uk)

Best Man Speech Advice and pointers courtesy of www.lastnightoffreedom.co.uk

Buy a Suit Advice courtesy of www.suitmaker.co.uk

Cut-Throat Razor Advice courtesy of www.executive-shaving.co.uk

Wash the Windows Tony Glendinning, Window Cleaner

Break Down Door and Fireman's Lift Tony Glendinning, Fireman. (Yes, that's right, he's both.)

Used Car Greg Mills, Car Salesman

Arm Wrestle Neil Pickup, Twice European and World Middleweight Arm-Wrestling Champion

Make Bow and Arrow Pete Davidson, Longbow Expert (www.tradlongbows.co.uk)

Fire Bow and Arrow Mark Davis, Archery Instructor (www.aasinfo.demon.co.uk)

Toss a Caber, Rip a Phone Book and Carnival Hammer Geoff Capes, Athlete, Strongman and Prize-Winning Budgerigar Breeder

HOW DID IT COME TO THIS?

I managed to get away with being hapless for the best part of thirty years—and I would probably have got away with it for much longer had my pesky father-in-law not rumbled me one Sunday morning late last year.

Assisting me with a few routine DIY tasks around the house I'd just moved into, he suggested I bleed the radiator while he set about plumbing in the washing machine. His casual, matter-of-fact tone suggested that my task would present few problems; indeed, it implied that men bleed radiators for fun from the age of twelve onwards.

He soon knew better, thanks to my blank, gormless expression, and the fact I approached the task holding a hacksaw. The only reason he didn't say anything was because we both knew he didn't have to; he was well within his rights to assume his only daughter had married the village idiot's half-wit brother. Tragically, the more I thought about it, the more I realized that I'd reached almost thirty-two years of age without learning any of the most important, and basic, Man Skills.

Obviously I could send an email, set the video for a fortnight on Wednesday and download music I'd never listen to, but life's proper skills, the ones most dads know? Nope, absolutely no idea. Happily—for me, at least—I know I'm not alone. Nobody bothers to learn how to mow the lawn properly or steer through a skid any more, so almost every man I know is as hapless as wot I am. Or at least, as hapless as wot I *was*, because I've spent many months researching and writing the book you hold before you.

I'm not claiming I know every trick in the book. I don't, and I wouldn't fancy my chances of landing a light aircraft should the pilot pass out. But I *do* now have a far better understanding of how to wire a plug, carve a chicken, and change a baby's diaper without him pissing in my eye. Plus, I finally know that you don't bleed a radiator with a hacksaw, and by the end of this book, so will you.

My father-in-law still thinks I'm a hapless moron, but you can't have everything.

How To...
Shake Hands
Properly

There's more to it than just clamping onto the other guy's hand and holding on. Admittedly, not *much* more to it than that, but we wouldn't want you to make the wrong first impression and for him to think you're a sissy from the start, so follow the advice closely.

Shake a stranger's hand too firmly and he'll think you're trying to outmuscle him in a test of manhood that may later lead on to a bout of naked wrestling on the floor. Shake too limply and he'll dismiss you as a spineless cretin who's not to be trusted. The art is to find a happy balance, and the unwritten rules are simple...

The perfect handshake

Make eye contact, smile, or say 'hello', and extend your right hand, held at a slight downward angle.

Your grip should be firm but never fierce—this is not a test of brute force, so never *squeeze* his hand.

Shake using only your lower arm, and never bring your shoulder into play—that's when it becomes more physical; he'll sense testosterone.

Grip his hand for just two or three seconds, apply- ing a couple of short, controlled shakes to convey sincerity. (Movement of the hand is actually optional in a handshake, but if you don't move it up and down you're merely holding a strange man's hand. If we lived in a more open, tolerant society that would be fine, but we don't.)

Maintain eye contact throughout the shake and until the hands are withdrawn.

Assuming all's gone to plan, he'll think you're the kind of stand-up character he could happily employ, grant his daughter's hand in marriage to or just share some booze and fine cigars with long into the night. Possibly all three, if you've pulled off a really great shake.

The golden rules

- One handshake should fit all occasions: don't go changing it to suit different surroundings and people.
- The only time you should alter your approach is when shaking a woman's hand. Even then, simply lighten the grip slightly so as to not come across as some kind of frenzied sex pest.
- The two-handed shake is a nice touch, but 'a bit too familiar' for strangers. Save it for close friends and long-time associates only.
- Hold on too long and the other person will think you're particularly needy.
- But never snatch your hand back; that's just rude.
- Keep your body language open throughout the shake.
- Make sure your hands are dry.
- Never fidget as you shake.
- Don't wink, unless you're a cocky wanker.
- And never use the comedy hand-buzzer gag on strangers. Save it for your 'wacky' pals.

How To...
Buy Flowers

This is stupidly complicated, so concentrate a bit harder here.

The flowers you buy a woman have to be the right model for the right occasion. You might think wilting daffodils from the gas station or half a dozen cheap roses from the grocery store will suffice, but according to the mind-bogglingly complex Flower Rules For Men, you'd be very wrong indeed. Having seen only a tattered photocopy of these Rules, the following is a manly stab at making sense of it all...

Surprise her

If you only ever buy her flowers when you've done something wrong or want something unreasonable from her, she'll associate them with guilt. Get in the habit of buying her flowers for no reason whatsoever and they'll mean quite a bit more (and make you look good).

Romance

You can always play it safe with a nice bunch of red roses on Valentine's Day, just to prove once and for all that you have no imagination whatsoever. Or you could go for azaleas, tulips, violets, or bouquets of mixed flowers, which are all more imaginative and often less expensive. Not that money should be the issue where this special lady's concerned, of course.

Her birthday

You wouldn't want to get this wrong and ruin her big day, surely? If in doubt, a bouquet is your safest bet, and $70 is the approximate going rate for a decent bunch (at the time of going to press).

Your anniversary

If you married her, a good starting point is to first remember the correct date, then try to recall what flowers she had on her wedding day. You could scratch your chin for a while before buying the wrong thing, or you could ask one of her bridesmaids or just check your wedding photos to save time and money. A simple choice really.

Bad occasions

Good flowers for when bad stuff like deaths, amputations, and getting fired happen include (but are not limited to) forget-me-nots, statice and hydrangea. They suggest you're in touch with your sensitive side, even if you're not.

Get well

No real hard or fast rules here, apart from to make sure that if you're sending flowers to someone in hospital that they're allowed to have them on the ward. Don't send tulips as they wilt in the heat. And black roses, Nemophila Penny Black, or any other black flowers might convey the wrong sort of message.

New baby

According to The Rules, Gardenias = Joy = A Safe Bet.

Color-coded (for extra confusion)

If you're comfortable with the above and want to pretend you know flowers on a deeper level, be aware that their colors signify different things.

Red flowers equal passion, love, fire, and heat. Orange suggests fire and warmth, yellow is associated with spring, happiness, and sunshine.

Blue flowers suggest peace, serenity, and calm; purple equals luxury, splendor, and Elton John-esque opulence, while pink shouts femininity and grace and all that girly stuff.

White flowers denote purity, light, and innocence, while black, they claim, suggests style and enchantment (but also 'impending death' if delivered to an ailing retiree).

If in doubt, go for her favorite color, or something that matches the color of the room they're likely to be left to wither in.

And if you only read one thing on this page...

The most important of all Flower Rules For Men is: if in doubt, ask the nice lady behind the counter. As a woman, she'll happily ramble on at great length and will always know far more than you. Tell her the occasion, she'll work out all the complicated sub-texts and send you off with the right bunch.

How To...
Carve A Chicken (Or Turkey)
Like A Pro

Hack away at the bird aimlessly and you'll be left with a tiny little pile of scrap meat that you'd think twice about feeding a cat. Carve in the measured manner detailed below and you'll end up with fat slices of prime white poultry and several arched eyebrows...

Once cooked, take the bird out of the oven and let it cool, breast-side up, for at least fifteen minutes. This allows the fibers to relax, which makes carving through its flesh far easier, and which in turn clearly makes you look like you know what you're doing. Use a cutting board with a little trough around the edge so when you cut into the chicken its precious, tasty juices aren't wasted.

Once it has cooled take one very sharp, very flexible, thin-bladed carving knife, and a two-pronged carving fork (to steady the bird), and chop it up like so...

Step 1. Cut down between the leg and the breast. Pull the thigh away from the bird and cut through the joint to remove this choice dark meat—attempt to cut through the bone and you'll be there all day.

Step 2. To separate thigh from drumstick (the meat around the leg bone), cut through the ball and socket joint, then remove the opposite leg in a similar fashion. As a general rule, never buy a chicken if it has fewer or more than two legs.

Step 3. Before you can carve the big bits off the breast, make sure you remove the wishbone, otherwise it'll

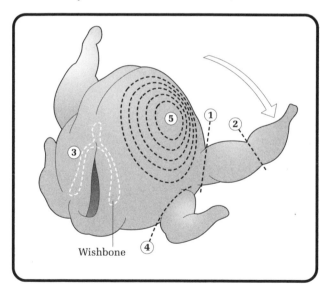

Wishbone

only get in the way and make things harder. To do this, loosen the skin from the flesh at the neck with your fingers, folding back the skin to expose the breastbone (the big bone that runs along the middle of the front). You should now be able to whip out that wishbone with a minimum of fuss.

Step 4. Cut horizontally above the wing joint and along through the breast—this makes it much easier to carve off the big juicy showpiece slices of meat in one.

Step 5. Finally, carve downward and parallel to the breastbone, going in as close to the bone as possible so as not to waste any precious meat. Repeat on the other side of the bone until you're left with a stripped carcass. Share the meat out amongst your hungry guests, serving with some potatoes and a nice gravy.

How To ...
Undo A Bra Using Only One Hand

In the hands of a horny novice, bra straps can maim and possibly even kill. That's not merely exagerrating for the purpose of a more dramatic introduction—it's based on the sorry tale of a young man who needed plastic surgery after catching a finger in the bra of his busty companion.

He was twenty-seven and knew no better (though he certainly should have by that age), and his injuries were serious enough for surgeons to suggest the introduction of Bra Camps for naive young men. Well, kind of. '[We] advocate patient self-education (during the adolescent years) on the mechanism of external female mammary support and postulate that it may be important in reducing the incidence of other such injuries,' claimed the *British Journal of Plastic Surgeons* in 2002.

Sadly, Bra Camps have not been forthcoming, and because you're attempting to unhook the external female mammary support with just the *one* hand, the following guide may just save your life...

Step 1. Along with a series of small hooks, tension in the bra strap keeps the garment tight—you'll need to isolate that tension before you can whip the bra clean off. Having slid your hand casually around her back, place thumb and fore-finger on the top, outer side of the bra strap, on either side of the locked hooks, with your three remaining fingers sliding underneath the bra strap.

Step 2. The three fingers should isolate the tension in the strap by pulling it away slightly from the woman's back, with the thumb and fore-finger gently squeezing together to release the hooks.

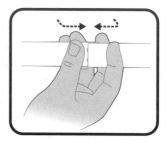

Step 3. If done properly, you should still be injury-free, the unhooked straps should fall down and the bra will be hang-ing free. If you need tips on what to do next, you'll need to buy a porn movie. That one with the

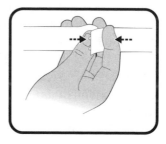

mustachioed man on the front comes highly recommended.

How To...
Start A Fire With Two Sticks

To be honest, where it says 'Two Sticks', it should probably read 'A Stick, A Stone, A Large Piece Of Board, Some Kindling, Another Stick And A Sore Arm', only that's not quite as snappy. This trick is also known as the bow and drill method, a nickname that would have also seen you reaching for the next page, so let's go with the Two Sticks. This technique takes time to prepare and an eternity to perfect, but apart from that it's a simple way of making an impressive Big Fire. This handy illustration shows the components involved...

The socket—an easy-to-grasp stone or piece of hardwood with a small indent in the center of the underside to hold the drill in place as you apply downward pressure.

The drill—this needs to be a straight, robust stick roughly 2 cm in diameter and about 20 cm long. The top end should be rounded, enabling it to fit snugly into the socket's indent, and the bottom end must be more pointed to generate more friction.

The fireboard—this can be any size you like, though a seasoned (dried) softwood board at least 5 cm wide, 15 cm long, and 2 cm thick is the preferred choice of most bushmen. You'll need to cut a depression close to the edge on one side of the board, big enough to accommodate the bottom of the drill. On the underside, whittle a V-shaped cut from the edge of the board to the depression (see illustration). This V-shaped notch should cut a small hole into the base of the depression, just big enough to allow the powder you'll produce to drop through to the kindling (see the illustration again, and look very closely). We're getting ahead of ourselves here. Keep concentrating hard and read on.

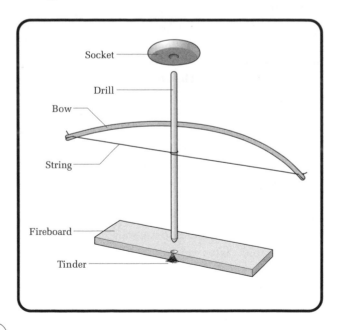

Socket

Drill

Bow

String

Fireboard

Tinder

The bow—this needs to be about 2.5 cm in diameter, and robust enough not to snap the moment you tie string to either end and bend it into shape. Simply cut a notch at either end of the stick, about an inch or so deep. Feed string through one notch and fasten with a knot, then bend the wood into a bow shape and secure with a second knot. Tie tight enough for the stick to stay bent.

After constructing the bow and drill, but before you begin the funny sawing motion, you'll need to collect a nice big pile of wood and kindling—if, after all your exertions, you end up with a flame but no wood to burn, you're more stupid than you look. (See page 133, How To…Build A Fire.)

Now, shove a bundle of finely-shredded kindling (which can be dead grass, leaves—anything dry that will burn) under the V-shaped cut in the fireboard, place one foot firmly on the board to keep it steady, then loop the bow-string over the drill shaft (see illustration), making sure the tension is firm. Position the drill in the pre-cut depression in the board, place the socket on top, held down with one hand, and you're all set.

Press down on the drill and move the bow from side to side using a steady horizontal sawing motion. As the motion becomes smoother, apply more downward pressure on the socket and work the bow faster. Saw as fast as your fat little fingers will go, then a bit faster still.

Eventually, after what may well seem like four days of this repetitive and tedious exertion, your sawing motion should grind the wood into a hot black powder. When the powder falls down onto the kindling, the heat should eventually provide a spark. Blow gently on the kindling until it ignites, and protect it from the wind as you move it towards your pre-prepared fire. Introduce it to the fire's kindling (dry twigs and leaves) and nurture until it rages nicely. The feeling should return to your arm after a few hours, and you should get faster with practice.

An alternative method for making a fire

The convex lens method won't make your hands bleed and requires you only to lie still for a while. It's only an option on a bright, sunny day, and you'll need the lens on a pair of binoculars, a camera, or a magnifying glass for it to work. Angle said lens so that it directs the sun's rays onto a small pile of kindling. Hold in place until the kindling starts to smolder and gently blow on it to turn the smoldering into a flame. Apply it to your pre-prepared fire and wonder why you ever bothered making fire with two sticks.

How To...
Beat A Hangover

When you finally wake up in a pool of stagnant dribble, your head will be pounding and you'll stink of cheap booze and smoke. If you have work today, you're in trouble, not to mention late. If it's the weekend and you're free to sit around all day in your underwear, you'll still want to shake the bastard behind your eyes as quickly as possible. Before detailing The Miracle Cure, however, a brief scientific explanation as to why you're feeling so crappy. (Not that you'll care at this moment...)

Brief scientific explanation
It's either the cogeners (impurities) in your alcohol or it's the ethanol, a toxic fog coughed up by your liver as it breaks down the booze. Either way, you're miserable, so best we skip the bit about vasopressin and methanol and head straight onto The Miracle Cure...

The Miracle Cure
Sorry, we've just checked again and there is no miracle cure. The only way to avoid a hangover is to drink in moderation or abstain completely, neither of which are any fun at all. Alternatively, you could continually

increase your alcohol tolerance, thereby keeping one step ahead of the hangover, but a book as responsible as this would advise against that. So, your only hope is to limit the damage as much as possible.

Before you start boozing

Eat fatty food and drink milk to line your stomach. This slows the absorption of booze into your bloodstream, giving your body time to process the toxins in the liquor more effectively.

If you can limit yourself to one drink per hour, your body should be able to process the alcohol and keep you on an even keel. One. Per hour. And even then this is based on drinking beer; hard liquor will make a mockery of this advice.

The darker the drink, the greater the chance of you waking up with a throbbing head. Cogeners give drinks their different colors and tastes, but as toxins they also poison your body and leave you in a sorry heap.

And never mix your drinks, particularly not the dark ones. Toxins combined gang up to do far more damage.

Drink water between drinks, even if it's on the sly in the toilet. Alcohol is a diuretic, which means your body will make you piss out every last drop of water instead of sending it to the various vital organs that need water to function properly. Deprived of water, your brain will shrink and you'll wake up feeling like death.

Bubbly drinks and tonic may seem like a wise alternative to a steady diet of beer, but they're not. They've been scientifically proven to speed up the alcohol absorption into your system, plus they rot your teeth and make you flabby.

As a rule, bottled beer has higher alcohol content than pints, primarily because the bartender can't get at it to water it down and make it go further. Not all bartenders do this, just the unscrupulous bastards. And they know who they are.

And when you stagger in with puke in your hair and chilli sauce down your front, remember to drink more water before passing out in a heap. It will help rehydrate you, although you're still going to feel like shit in about four hours...

The next day [about four hours later]

Having ignored all of the above, you wake up feeling like shit. Your only hope now is to hope one of the following 'hangover cures' actually works. You have nothing to lose...

Sleep— As long as possible. It might go away.

Vitamins A, B and C— The body loses all three as you guzzle booze. Replace in tablet or food forms as soon as possible. Vitamin A is found in eggs and carrots, B in bananas and chilli peppers and C in all good citrus fruits.

Coffee or Cola— Caffeine helps reduce the swelling of blood vessels in your brain, although it will also dehydrate you and make matters worse unless you glug water as well.

A canary— According to the ancient Romans (who knew a thing or two about debauchery), a canary for breakfast works wonders. They'd fry him, probably in olive oil, although grilling is considered far healthier.

Ginger— Grated into orange juice or taken in pill form, this has been known to work well on upset stomachs.

Chocolate— Your body uses up its sugar supply breaking down the booze. You'll need to replace it asap.

Exercise— Jumping up and down helps send blood and oxygen to your shrivelled brain, while the sweat flushes the toxins out of your body. Sex also helps, apparently.

Half a lemon— According to Puerto Rican booze fans, if you rub the halved lemon under your drinking arm you'll be feeling 100 percent within the hour.

Burnt toast— The carbon is good for soaking up the poisonous toxins floating around your body, although it tastes like shit.

Bananas—Contain magnesium, potassium, and sugar, which are lost as you drink.

Raw cabbage— Helps cure a headache. Germans swear by sauerkraut juice to replace lost nutrients.

Menudo soup— The Mexican alternative, available in a can and containing tripe, dried maize, and pigs' feet. Yes, puking your guts up can also make you feel better.

Take one or more of the above, lie down with the curtains closed, and wait for the room to settle. Keep waiting and eventually you'll feel better, then you'll accept that you're getting older and can't shake it off like you used to. You'll tell yourself that booze abuse is a young man's game and vow never to imbibe so greedily ever again. You can shake your head all you like, though, because you're fooling no one.

How To...
Crack Open A Coconut

You're right, clanking it against a sturdy wall or brick would do the job, but such a ham-fisted approach would guarantee most of the lovely juice inside the nut is wasted. So, this technique is for the controlled, idiot-proof approach...

Step 1. Rest the coconut in the middle of one hand, with the tip at one end and the 'eyes' at the other. If you have a bowl to hand, hold the coconut over it to catch the juice.

Step 2. Find a blunt implement–the back of a knife or a heavy stone—and bang the coconut around its center, rotating the seed until it gently starts to split open. As the crack widens, pour the juice into your bowl or straight down your trap. Once the juice has drained, to get to the flesh continue knocking at the coconut shell until it opens. You should be left with two even halves, but no one's measuring.

Step 3. To reach the juice without splitting the nut open, hammer a sharp tip into the 'eyes' of the nut— a nail or sharp stone should suffice. Insert a straw and you've turned that coconut into a tall drink to be sipped at leisure. If you've been washed up on a deserted island, however, you may struggle for a straw so should skip this altogether.

How To...
Master The
Fireman's Lift (And Carry)

Firefighters are incredibly manly and they do a marvellous job, hats off to each and every one of them, and so on and so forth. However, it's impossible to expect them to be on hand at the start of every emergency. Sometimes they're otherwise engaged drinking beer or putting out a small trash can fire, which is why you may need to know how to cart someone to safety in the unlikely event of a fire.

The victim here has been overcome by the smoke and fumes or is just too injured to hobble to safety after a large pot of glue landed awkwardly on their leg during the commotion, or what have you. You're first on the scene and have just read the following instructions...

The lift and carry

The lift is easier if you have an accomplice to help pick him (or her) up. However, assuming you don't, you'll need to struggle the victim up and onto his feet as best you can. He should be facing you, with your right leg bent at the knee and advanced between his thighs, with your weight on that front foot.

With his weight resting on your right thigh, grip the victim's right hand with your left and place your right arm under his crotch and round the back of his right thigh (see figure 1). If you're playing the hero by rescuing a woman, your hand should go around the outside and rear of her thighs, in case she wakes up and finds you fumbling around where you shouldn't be.

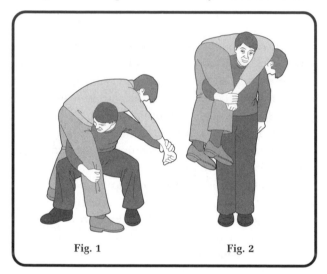

Fig. 1   Fig. 2

Bending at the knees and using his right arm as a lever, pull the victim up and over your 'leading' shoulder, distributing his weight as evenly as possible and using your legs to bear the weight to avoid pulling your back. Be aware that it's only a proper fireman's carry if the victim is carried across both shoulders—dispersing their weight will let you carry them further and with minimum disruption to their potentially injured body.

Stand as tall as possible, bending your head forward slightly to minimize your discomfort (figure 2), and slowly stagger off to somewhere safer, like over there.

Taking sides

If you've gone that extra yard by clambering heroically up a ladder and through a window to save your victim, the side of the window your ladder is resting on determines over which shoulder you carry the person. If you're right-handed, you'll naturally favor your right shoulder for bearing the brunt of the weight, so should therefore pitch your ladder alongside the right of the window. This ensures the victim's head is less likely to clank violently against the window frame as you clamber back out. If your ladder is pitched on the left, remember to adjust these instructions accordingly—and whichever side you approach from, be careful on the way back down.

How To...
Bleed A Radiator

An expert on this kind of thing would advise you to bleed your radiators at least twice a year, then when you ignore their advice charge you $250 to fix them and only accept cash.

Thanks to this entry, you'll now be able to tell him where to stick his hourly rate and bleed it yourself, for it's a stupidly simple procedure. For 'bleed the radiator', read 'drain your central heating system of any air that's made its way in.'

Air in your heating system is a common problem and nothing to be ashamed about. As you heat and cool water, air bubbles are released. That air rises to the highest part of the heating system—normally your radiator—and displaces some of the water, and because air doesn't conduct heat anywhere near as efficiently as water you'll soon notice the difference in temperature. Left inside, the air will dramatically reduce the amount of heat your radiator emits until one day you wake to find an Eskimo catching fish at the end of your bed.

The telltale sign of when a radiator needs bleeding is if, when the heating is on, the top part is noticeably colder than the bottom—this suggests there's a little air trapped inside. If it's cool from top to bottom, you've just got a lot more air to bleed dry. OK, the science portion of the lesson is over, here's how you bleed...

Step 1. Turn the central heating off at the thermostat and allow the water to cool. Then, insert a bleed key into the bleed valve—which is the little screwy nub thing normally located at the top end of the radiator, or sometimes around the back. Before turning the key, wrap an old rag around it to catch any dirty water which might spurt out onto the carpet, or on those smart new pants of yours.

Step 2. Give the bleed valve a good half-turn counter-clockwise until you hear a hissing sound—don't be overly alarmed, that's just the sound of the air escaping.

Step 3. When the hissing stops, the air has escaped, at which point some dirty water should spurt out into the rag. That's your cue to close the valve by turning it back to its original position—a half-turn clockwise, should you be struggling to keep up.

Step 4. Remove scarf and gloves, bask in the warmth of a job well done, and make a note to do it again in six months' time.

How To...
Communicate Using Morse Code

Morse code was one of the earliest forms of text messaging, dreamt up by Samuel Morse in the 1830s to let his boss know he wouldn't be coming in today because he was coming down with flu although it turned out to be nothing more than a mild man-cold that soon passed, but his boss didn't need to know that.

Still popular to this day among salty sea dogs, Morse code breaks down the twenty-six letters of the alphabet, the numbers 1 to 9, and various punctuation marks into a series of simple dots and dashes, traditionally transmitted by radio pulses.

For the man who rarely ventures out to sea, however, the code can just as easily be transmitted by torch light to your buddy across the road, or to Mr. Wong at Wok This Way. He doesn't deliver, of course, but I can't do anything about that.

The Code
A dot indicates a short pulse of light or sound, and a dash a longer one.

A . –	
B – ...	1 . – – – –
C – . – .	2 .. – – –
D – ..	3 ... – –
E .	4 .... –
F .. – .	5 .....
G – – .	6 – ....
H	7 – – ...
I ..	8 – – – ..
J . – – –	9 – – – – .
K – . –	0 – – – – –
L . – ..	Full stop . – . – . –
M – –	Comma – – .. – –
N – .	Colon – – – ...
O – – –	Question mark .. – – ..
P . – – .	Exclamation mark – . – . – –
Q – – . –	Apostrophe . – – – – .
R . – .	Hyphen – .... –
S ...	Fraction symbol – .. – .
T –	Quotation mark . – .. – .
U .. –	Equals sign – ... –
V ... –	Ignore the previous word
W . – –	(it was a mistake) ....
X – .. –	(eight dots)
Y – . – –	
Z – – ..	

The dash is normally three times as long as the dot. A word of warning, though: be sure to leave a sufficient delay between transmitting each letter, otherwise it'll produce either a continuous, ear-splitting noise or a randomly flashing light, which may give the impression you're just having a party.

Test your knowledge!

The first successful transmission using Morse code was on 6 January 1838, when Morse and his pioneering sidekick Alfred Vail sent a message three miles down a wire. It read:

`- / --- ..- .-.- - / -- .- / ..../`
`-. --- / .- .- - .. . -. -  .-- .- .. - . .-. i s`
`N o L o s e r stop`

Yes, you will have to work it out yourself. You've been taking *Man Skills* for granted.

A Patient Waiter is no Loser.

How To...
Give A Best Man's Speech

Unless you're some kind of social delinquent, at some point in your life you'll probably be asked to stand up and say a few kind words about a close friend and his newly wed wife. There's no right or wrong way to do this, but there are many ways of making a fool of yourself. The following pointers should steer you in the right direction...

Tip 1. Fail to prepare...

...and prepare to make a complete and utter ass of yourself in front of a room full of his and her relatives. In the months leading up to the wedding, put together a loose skeleton of a speech, adding to it whenever you hear a half-decent anecdote that sounds about right, or you remember something from your childhood / school days / college life / et cetera that seems appropriate.

Eventually you'll have too many anecdotes, at which point you'll need to cast off the more unsavory narratives and prepare a final speech. Ideally, you should do this a few weeks before the wedding, giving you time to perfect the structure. By all means add a few creative tweaks right up to the moment you stand up, but avoid any last-minute re-writes—this will only cause you confusion. And you can ill afford that.

Also, don't make the mistake of thinking you can turn up on the day of the wedding and hit them with a little improv, effortlessly working the room like Jerry Seinfeld in his prime. You can't, and you will die on your feet in a funny suit you've been made to wear.

Tip 2. Start as you mean to go on

Your opening gambit is crucial if you're to pull this off. There are three possible angles of approach…

Safe-bet subjects

These include: the happy couple's unique magic…the way they sparkle together…all that kind of flowery crap the old people like…talk about the groom's amusing childhood stories…except any involving him discovering the magical powers of his front tail—that would be bad…stick with complementing the 'marvellous venue' and the 'lovely food'…compliment the bridesmaids, but don't leer or wink inappropriately…in short, just say nice things about all the nice people and offend nobody.

Thin-ice subjects

Talk about how the couple first met, providing he didn't have her shipped over from Bangkok in a box …mention the groom's embarrassing habits, but keep them of the non-genital variety…and look ahead to the honeymoon, that should be safe enough, you'd think…

Ice breakers

Don't mention what really went on at the bachelor party or produce photographic evidence and receipts to back up your claims...don't discuss his or her previous partners and all the stuff they did together... don't, at any point, start a sentence with the phrase: 'My mother-in-law...'...say nothing negative about the food or the venue, even if they offered very poor value for money...and don't make fun of the bridesmaids, at least not out loud...

Tip 3. The delivery

Tragically, the tone and delivery you're looking for is the Hugh Grant character in the loveable flick *Four Weddings and a Funeral*—inoffensive charm delivered by a floppy-haired, upper-crust buffoon. Choose your content wisely, then follow these simple pointers:

- Prompt cards are fine, though any more than four or five might be a bit excessive.
- A good length for the speech depends on what's gone before it. You'll most likely be delivering your speech after the groom's brief introduction and the bride's father's drunken ramble; if they've both blathered on at length you may need to trim yours down as you go, as people can only feign attention for so long. If they both nervously whipped through theirs in double-quick time, you may be better off adding an extra anecdote or two—the crowd will want their money's worth even if they didn't pay to get in.

- Avoid excess alcohol before the speeches. A little liquid courage is fine, a drunken fool with soup down his front is less fine.
- Work the crowd by maintaining eye contact and sweeping the room. This projects confidence, even if you're so nervous you could pass out.
- To keep the tone lively, try to inflect some form of expression in your voice, particularly at the start and end of each line. A monotone delivery will have people reaching for the gin.
- Be yourself and avoid the pompous little touches you think the event demands—leave all that 'Ladies and Gentlemen' crap at home. Use your natural speaking voice and normal mannerisms, and remember that the groom picked you because of who you are rather than who you can pretend to be. Impersonations of famous people are ill-advised, unless you can do them really well. Even then, it's questionable. No one likes a cocky best man, or worse, an impressionist.
- Visual gimmickry can help keep people's attention while they're drinking themselves into a light stupor. An amusing poster or suitable item of clothing can both work, a PowerPoint presentation is inexcusable.
- Avoid in-jokes, unless you want to lose 98 percent of the guests when you ramble on about badger-baiting in Soho.
- Most important of all, remember that the vast majority of the crowd doesn't want you to

make a complete ass of yourself. Hear them laugh at things which aren't even remotely funny and you'll realize they want you to do well. Why, they admire your balls for getting up in the first place and have no idea that you drunkenly begged the groom to get someone else to do it. Ah well, it's too late now. Just get up there, do your thing, then you can drink until you can no longer see.

How To...
Hit A Carnival Hammer
(And Make The Bell Ring)

No self-respecting carnival should be allowed to open its gates without first having installed one of those test-of-strength hammer contraptions, and no self-respecting male should be allowed to visit a carnival without knowing how to make the weight scuttle up the pin and make the bell ring. With the world's smallest goldfish riding on it, failure is not an option.

The uninitiated man normally attempts to hit the target with all the might he can muster, not unreasonably thinking that raw power will bring success. But as his veins bulge, his hands blister and the weight climbs all of 10 centimeters, this man can only shuffle off shamefaced, muttering under his breath about the carnies having rigged the machine.

The skilled man understands that the difference between success and failure here is not brute force, but hand-eye coordination. A weak man who hits the target spot-on stands a far better chance of ringing the bell than a muscular freak who lands his hammer hard on the edge of the target.

If you're in any position to practice, trade power for accuracy until your eye is 'in', then concentrate on applying as much power and speed through the swing as your frame allows, without ever ceding accuracy. Swing over your shoulder or around your waist, whichever allows for a better strike.

To separate the men from the boys, some carnivals use longer pins, which require a more powerful blow to send the weight scuttling up to the top. Your best bet here is to prepare by working on your biceps and bulking up on steroids so that your neck thickens and your genitals shrivel. Or alternatively, know when you're beaten and try the ring toss instead. (In which case, see page 151, How To...Throw Properly.)

How To...
Drink A Yard
Of Beer

If you're a fan of binge drinking—and these days, who isn't?—then you'll want to do it properly by downing four pints of a beer of your choice from a long glassy shaft in one swift drink.

The Yard of Ale has been around since at least 1685, when noted English scribe John Evelyn wrote about 'his Majesty's health being drunk in a flint glass of a yard long.' If his majesty himself took part in such debauched revelry it isn't recorded, but the act quickly caught on among stagecoach drivers, back when horse-drawn carriages were the quickest means of travel. So lazy that they couldn't be bothered to climb down from their seat above the carriage, the yard glass could be passed straight up to them. They drained it in one gulp, started up the horses and drove away, often careering off into crowds of innocent peasants.

So the yard glass was basically an invention to help people drive drunk in the olden times. Best we conveniently ignore that fact and press on with the instructions...

The instructions

The obvious problem is that your gut wasn't designed to down four pints of booze in one hearty swig, so you'll end up drinking beer through both nostrils until you master the technique. Luckily, it's not all that difficult. All you need to be aware of is the infamous 'air rush.' This occurs when you tip the vessel up as you drink—the displaced booze is replaced by an air pocket which rushes down to the bottom of the yard and forces the remaining beer down the flute and towards your gut at great speed. This can be prevented by using one of two foolproof techniques.

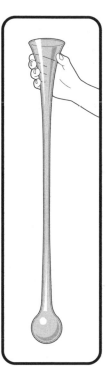

Technique 1. The simplest of the two is to ignore the baying crowd and drink slowly but surely. Tilt the glass very, very steadily until it's emptied to the point where air can enter slowly and safely—thus avoiding that air rush. Your manhood will be questioned if you're still drinking twenty minutes later, but at least your slacks will stay dry.

Technique 2. The second option is far more of a crowd-pleaser. Drain the yard as normal, but give the impression you're a seasoned pro by slowly twirling the glass in a clockwise direction once you reach the bulb. Because the twisting motion releases the air pressure gently, you'll again avoid that late wave of air and reach the end unscathed. With experience, you'll be able to tilt the shaft more sharply, allowing you to finish your yard in a better time.

For now, raise your hand in triumph, wipe the suds from your chin and try not to vomit down your leg.

Speed supping

According to the book of *Guinness World Records*, the fastest recorded gulping of a Yard of Ale was by British boozer Peter Dowdeswell. He drank his 1.42 liters (just 2.5 pints, mind) in 5 seconds on May 4, 1975. In 1955, while a Rhodes scholar at University College, Oxford, Australian Prime-Minister-to-be Bob Hawke set the standard for his countrymen by consuming the same volume of subsidized ale in 11 seconds, putting himself in the *Guinness World Records* book at the same time. And all at the taxpayer's expense. Nice.

How To...
Tie A Bow Tie

Let's assume, for argument's sake, that at some point in your life you'll move in the type of circles where a bow tie is required. Now, you could always buy a clip-on and save yourself the bother of reading this chapter and of tying yourself in knots, but clip-ons are for posers and morons. Do it properly, like so...

Step 1. Here's a nice looking bow tie, drawn as you'd see it in the mirror. The left end, as you see it, should be about 4 cm lower than the right end.

Step 2. Cross the longer length over the shorter end.

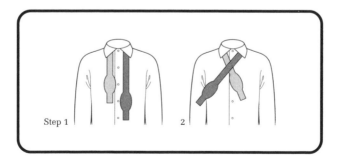

Step 1   2

Step 3. Feed the longer end up through the loop.

Step 4. Now, take the shorter end and form the front loop of your bow by doubling it up and placing it across your shirt's collar points (the pointy bits on your, well, collar).

Step 5. Holding that front loop with the thumb and forefinger of your left hand, allow the long end to drop down over the front. You'll notice that this baby's almost effortlessly taking shape now.

Step 6. Holding it all in place, double the long end back on itself. Poke that long end through the loop behind the tie, even up the ends, and tighten.

Step 7. You're all done and you'll look even smarter when you put some pants on.

How To...
Mow The Lawn

Lawn mowing gets a bad rep, and rightly so—it's a tedious pain in the ass and it takes up your whole weekend. So, the following tips have been assembled to help make the whole process as painless as possible. They won't win you any horticultural awards but at least you'll have a nice, greenish patch of grass to sit on...

Tip 1. Buy a decent mower, preferably one with a box to catch the clippings, which will take the strain off your back. Cylinder mowers give more distinct and lasting strips and are good for cutting those fancy football-field stripes all men admire. Keep the blades sharp at all times for a cleaner cut.

Tip 2. If you've allowed it to become a shabby, overgrown garden, poke a big stick into the undergrowth before you begin to make sure there are no rocks or moles hiding in there. Both will mangle the blades on your new mower, and you won't be able to take it back because you've already lost the receipt.

Tip 3. Always cut an overgrown garden down in stages. This allows the roots to recover between cuts.

Lop it off with one stroke and they'll weaken, go into shock and whimper a bit before dying on you—and then it really will look shabby. Also, never make the mistake of thinking that if you buzz the lawn as low as it can go, you won't have to cut it so soon again next time—you'll actually be pulling the roots too close to the surface and exposing them to damaging sunlight.

Tip 4. How low should you go? Good question. This varies, depending on how much it rains and how fast the grass grows and what have you, but a general guide is just over a centimeter in the summer to 2 centimeters in winter. If kids and dogs are likely to trample all over it, keep the grass a little longer to protect it from wear and tear. If you only plan on using it to read the newspaper on Sunday mornings, you can afford to take it down a little more. But be warned: a certified expert who knows what he's talking about would tell you that cutting more than one-third of the height of the grass in any one session will seriously damage those precious roots.

Tip 5. To make your lawn look as healthy as possible during the summer months, feed it a lawn fertilizer in late spring. Follow the instructions on the packet and expect greener, thicker turf that's free of weeds and moss.

Tip 6. During hot spells, let the grass grow a little longer and mow less often. Don't feed or water it, even if it starts to turn brownish—you'll encourage the grass to root closer to the surface, which can cause long-term damage in the fierce heat.

Tip 7. Never mow when the grass is wet or frosty. You won't get a good, even cut and are more likely to spread fungus around.

Tip 8. When the conditions do finally allow you to mow, vary the direction to stop the grass getting lazy and leaning to one side after several cuts. A shaggy lawn just looks shoddy, so keep those wily blades on their toes.

Tip 9. Finally, when trimming the edges of your lawn, lay a plank of wood along the perimeter to give you a nice straight edge, and a thick, heavy rope along the edge of curvy borders. Use clippers on the edges for a more professional finish, or trick a young person into doing the job if you can no longer be bothered. Frankly, you deserve to put your feet up for a while.

How To...
Change A Diaper

Sadly, there's only so long you can ignore the noxious waft from a soiled diaper in the hopes that it'll just go away. It won't, so you'll have to clean up the mess yourself for a change. A baby's output is nothing short of staggering—on average, he'll fill fifteen diapers to the brim every day and take pride in refilling it the minute you've changed him. The only saving grace is that the diaper changing is relatively easy if you're using disposables, so use these and conveniently ignore the fact they're not as environmentally friendly as cloth diapers (but then, you don't have to wash them).

Mothers generally change diapers after a feeding or when 'putting them down'—code for 'putting them to sleep'. You could experiment for yourself as to when the best time for a change is, or you could save time and trouble by accepting that all mothers know best.

To change him, find a flat surface, such as on the carpet or on a changing table. If you're working up high, keep one hand on his belly, otherwise he'll roll or crawl off towards danger and leave you to take the blame.

Step 1. Place him on his back, with your replacement diaper unfurled underneath him so that if he decides to backfire everywhere it's not going all over your white carpet. (A similar damage-prevention tip is to place a tissue over his front tail, otherwise he may unleash his party piece and piss in your eye.) Make sure the end of the diaper with the sticky tabs is under his back.

Step 2. Undo the soiled diaper, retch at the pungent horror, then use the clean sections of the diaper to wipe away any mess left on the baby. Grab both his ankles with one hand, raise his backside to the roof and remove the diaper. Fold securely and place out of his reach, to be disposed of later.

Step 3. Now, use baby wipes to clean what mess remains, taking care to get into any creases. Check for any rashes and apply a diaper-rash cream if required. If left to irritate your baby, the rash will wake him in the middle of the night, and then he'll wake you by screaming at the top of his lungs. If that happens, you'll wish you'd paid attention to this advice.

Remember to only ever wipe the baby from front to back, especially if he's a girl, otherwise you risk spreading the bacteria that can cause urinary tract infections, and nobody wants that.

Step 4. Having patted him dry, lower him onto that clean diaper, pull the front section through his legs and and seal it all together at the sides with the sticky tabs. Dispose of the dirty diaper in a special diaper bag or bin as quickly as humanly possible.

Step 5. Finally, wash your hands and wait a full five minutes until he needs changing again.

Some handy tips (from women)

Gather all of your diaper-changing kit around you before you begin and ensure it's all within easy reach, otherwise you'll have to leave the baby unattended, and you've been warned about his wandering ways.

Never change him on a cold surface, he'll wail like a banshee for hours. Place a changing mat or a cloth beneath him for added comfort and warmth.

Distract a struggling baby with a bright toy, but only when you're making the final fasten on the diaper. Use the same toy all the time and throughout the whole changing process and the baby will see through your sorry charade in no time and start acting up again.

When fastening the diaper, if you stick the tabs onto the baby's skin he'd be well within his rights to punch you. And if you notice marks around his legs and waist when you change him, slacken off a little next time or the social services might come calling.

How To...
Skim A Stone
Across Water

This is the one trick guaranteed to impress small children and women, but only if your skim bounces at least half a dozen times. Anything less is a waste of everyone's time.

The good news is that a team of French scientists investigated stone-skimming and discovered that it all comes down to the kinematic viscosity of the water, which is pretty much what we all suspected. However, they also found out that $\frac{1}{2}MV^2\mathrm{x}[N] - \frac{1}{2}MV^2\mathrm{x}[0] = -N\mu Mgl$, which was quite a shock, certainly to me. Anyway, in layman's terms, it seems your chances of a double-figure skim are increased significantly by following several simple rules...

Rule 1. The water should be as still as possible, for obvious reasons, while the stone should be flat and circular to encourage more bounce.

Rule 2. A common misconception in this game is that to muster enough power for a double-figure spin, you'll need to throw the stone as hard as physically possible. Speed of entry into the water does count, but only when it's combined with spin. This stabilizes the stone through the water and maximizes the number of bounces you'll achieve.

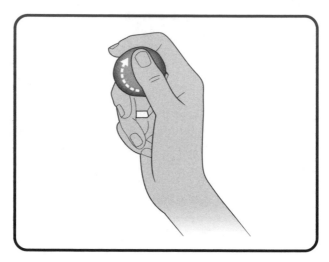

On releasing the stone, spin it in a clockwise direction, or counterclockwise if you're left handed.

Rule 3. The perfect angle of entry is exactly 20 degrees. Anything less and it will lose much of its energy dragging through the water, and anything more than 45 degrees and it won't bounce, just sink. Like a stone.

Rule 4. You'll need to spin the sucker more than 14 times per second and skim faster than 12 m^{s-1} to come close to the current world record of 40 skips, established by Kurt Steiner in 2003. m^{s-1}? Nope, no idea either. Just concentrate on spinning the stone with your index finger as you release it. Flick it in a clockwise direction (if you're right-handed) to increase its speed of rotation. The greater the flick, the greater the rotation and sure enough, the greater the skim.

How To...
Fight A Raging Fire*

First, a timely caveat. Everyone knows Big Fires should be avoided at all costs. At the first sign of a giant blaze you should book it outside and call the fire department. However, a small blaze in, say, a frying pan can be extinguished with a minimum of fuss...

Step 1. Under no circumstances should you attempt to move the pan: that oil is both boiling and burning and liable to cause you great pain.

Step 2. Instead, if you can safely reach the controls without leaning over the pan, turn the stove off. (If you can't, accept defeat and call the fire department.)

Step 3. Resist the urge to throw water over the flames; oil and water don't mix and you'll create a fireball accompanied by a small explosion. I know it sounds cool; don't do it anyway.

Step 4. Drape a fire blanket carefully over the pan.

Step 5. No, I've no idea what a fire blanket is or

where you'd find one either, so run a dish towel (or cloth) under a tap, wring it out fully, and cover the pan with that instead.

Step 6. The flames should die down. Leave the pan to cool completely, make yourself a sandwich, and learn these fire prevention tips by heart:

- I must never fill my pan more than one-third full.
- I must dry all food before introducing it to hot oil–any water may make the oil explode.
- I should take smoking oil as a warning sign that it's too hot. I will turn it off and let it cool.
- I should never ever leave a frying pan unattended, not even to tell the Jehovah's Witnesses at the door where to stick their Bible.
- I will always be asleep between 10 p.m. and 4 a.m., aware that most house fire incidents happen between those hours, mainly when drunken morons decide they want French fries.

Warning: The fire department advises against you fighting a fire, unless it's a small one that can be brought under control by an untrained civilian. Only approach fires with extreme caution. And consider yourself warned.

How To...
Buy A Suit That Actually Looks Good On You

If you're the type of man who enjoys paying a small fortune to have his inner thighs felt up by a handsy old man, this entry is not for you. Take your dapper three-piece and skip on over to the next entry.

If you're the type of man who needs a decent suit but doesn't want to have to sell both kidneys on eBay to fund it, the following basic rules should hold you in good stead...

The head

The easiest but most important rule of all: make your own mind up. By all means consider the opinions of your yapping female companion who prefers you in violet, and the smarmy sales assistant who works on commission. The final decision, however, must always be yours. If it doesn't look and feel right to you, you've just wasted your money.

The jacket–plain or striped fabric?

Pinstripes come in thousands of combinations and suit bankers and real estate agents nicely, so let's discard that option right away. If in doubt, choose a plain fabric. It's generally more versatile and has quiet, understated efficiency. Checkered suits are another option, if you don't mind dressing like a clown.

Double- or single-breasted?

This is a matter of taste. Double-breasted are less common, somewhat retro, and most likely to be found on the male captain of the local golf team. He knows it makes him look distinguished as he escorts the ladies and other undesirables from the premises. Single-breasted is the safer option.

Arm holes

It's worth paying a little extra for a suit with two arm holes, and the basic rule is that they should be tight but comfortable. Hold both arms up over your head–if the material's too tight, the jacket will ride up and show off the back of your shirt, which is not good.

Cuffs

A good test to ensure correct cuff-length is to let your arms hang loose and then curl up your hands. If the jacket cuffs touch the middle of each palm, the length's about right. The amount of shirt you want showing beneath the cuff is up to you. A centimeter is considered just about right, unless you happen to be wearing brand-new cufflinks you desperately want to show off, in which case just less than 4 cm is more like it.

Length of jacket

This varies depending on your shape, but as a general guide, a regular suit jacket should be about level with the top of your buttocks.

Vents

A finishing touch to be found at the rear of the jacket. Vents help slim the upper body and come in three options: a single vent in the center, one on either side, or none at all.

No vents—Suits the thin man by allowing the jacket to naturally hang straight at the sides and widen his scrawny profile.

Single vent—The most popular option, designed for the average-build man carrying a little baggage around the midriff. The vent encourages the jacket to stretch and sit more comfortably, reducing unsightly lumps and bumps. The vent also makes the bottom of the jacket flair slightly on either side, giving the impression you're fairly well defined in the chest area.

Twin vents—Best for chunky monkeys. They ensure the suit sits more comfortably, giving the impression of a slimmer stomach and a more defined chest, and could well save you from death by suffocation.

Lapels

You can judge a man by his lapel.

Medium lapel—The safety-first default setting, for the man who doesn't want to make any bold statements.

Thin lapel—Works best on trim men, particularly trim men who want to display a more flamboyant, individual streak.

Wide lapel—This man has a slightly retro, wild-at-heart streak. It's probably a cry for help and shouldn't ever be worn to a job interview.

The lapel can also be used to lengthen or shorten your upper body. A long, thin lapel (teamed with one or two front buttons on the jacket and plain, flat-fronted trousers) will lengthen the upper body—good news for stocky men with short upper bodies (soldiers, football players and bouncers), and men with large upper bodies who want to appear a little slimmer.

Pants

Obviously it's beneficial if they're cut from the same cloth as the jacket, and when you stand bolt upright the legs should rest on the tops of your shoes and crease 5 or 6 centimeters higher. That's officially a snug fit.

Crotch

As a general rule, you need enough room to put your hands in your pockets without discomfort. If you can play pocket pool without disrupting the fabric, they're too big. If your mini-me is visible beneath the fabric every time you sit down, you need a more generous cut.

Pleats and turned-up hems

Both very popular in the 1980s, therefore to be avoided at all costs. And here's a free tip for the vertically challenged: non-pleated, plain-fronted, straight-legged slacks without turned-up hems will create the appearance of longer, thinner legs. Obviously, for gangly, tall guys wishing to look a little more compact the opposite applies, and pleats and turned-up hems are sadly back in style.

How To...
Start A Frozen Car
In Winter Weather

If your car has frozen overnight it almost certainly won't start, which means you won't be able to get in to work today and can spend your day learning How To...Become A Multi-Millionaire In Five Working Days (Or Your Money Back)—see page 234.

If you're still reading, you clearly have no choice but to make it into work today for some important presentation or other, or to deliver a package to someone several miles away, or some other such scenario. So, for those who need to start a car in freezing conditions, here's what to do...

Plan ahead

A big freeze will sap the car battery's power, rendering it completely useless. If the weatherman predicts a cold front moving in overnight (let's say 14°F), whip out your car's battery the night before, having first consulted your car manual on how that can be done most safely. Bring the battery indoors and wrap a blanket around it to show that you really care. If you're really serious about getting to work every day in Arctic conditions, it would also help if you changed to a lightweight winter oil, rather than a heavier oil which can hinder engine efficiency.

Damage limitation

If you ignore all of the above and wake to find your car has frozen, the quickest way to defrost it is by attaching a hose to the exhaust of a working car and feeding the other end under the engine of your vehicle. Once warmed back to life, the engine should be easier to start. Even so, make sure the heater, radio, all the lights, and anything else that will sap the battery's energy are all switched off before you turn the ignition key.

Turning tricks

Turn and hold the key for five to ten seconds, but if it's an older car (and therefore a non-fuel-injected model), you'll need to give it just a little gas—a few pumps will suffice, but don't overdo things. If it's fuel-injected, the clever computer chip running the injectors will find an optimum gas flow to start the engine for you.

If it doesn't start, let the car rest for a couple of minutes before trying again—over-grinding the starter will cause mechanical damage that costs money to repair.

Pulling off

Finally, having followed all of the above, your engine has started. Do not drive straight off and floor it, flying away in a fog of smoke. Allow the engine to run for a couple of minutes until it's properly warmed up and the oil has moved through it. Cold oil coursing through the car can mess up your engine badly, thereby increasing your blood pressure. After a couple of minutes, put the car in gear and go about your business.

How To...
Open Champagne
(The Sophisticated, Unflustered Way)

If you've paid good money for swanky booze, the least you can do is open it properly and give the impression you drink this stuff all the time—although not to the point of it being a problem or anything.

However, before you even think about opening the champagne, make certain it's been in an ice bucket long enough to chill properly—it needs to be 45°F, according to the experts. Cool champagne tastes all wrong; warm champagne tastes even worse and is far more likely to foam and spill when you open the bottle, making you look like a fat-fingered idiot. Once chilled, you're ready to open and pour...

Step 1. Take a nice, crisp white cloth and dry off the bottle so you can get a better grip on it. Remove the foil from the top of the bottle, then loosen and remove the wire cage surrounding the cork. With the bottle upright, drape the cloth over the top—she'll think this looks professional; no need to mention it's there to catch the cork should it accidentally shoot out into her eye. With the cage removed, the pressure inside the bottle can sometimes force the cork out on its own and send it across the room at speeds of up to 180 mph. It's probably best to keep your thumb on the cork throughout.

Step 2. Lower the bottle so it's at a 45-degree angle, with the towel now draped over the neck of the bottle and concealing it from view. Hold the neck in one hand, with your thumb still firmly atop the cork. With your other hand, grip and very gently twist the bottle, *never the cork*. Keep turning slowly until you hear a gentle 'pop'—only impatient amateurs, racecar drivers, and rich bankers get the loud popping sound, which comes when the bubble-inducing carbon dioxide escapes from the bottle, followed by a hearty spurt of your expensive booze. Whip off the cloth, give the lady a knowing look, and prepare to pour. Having dedicated so much time and effort to uncorking the stupid thing, you'll need a suitable receptacle. Paper cups, chipped mugs, and those oversized beer steins are unsuitable and will undermine your work thus far. If this woman (or man, could be a man) means anything to you, invest in two tasteful champagne flutes.

Step 3. Unlike foaming ale, champagne doesn't require a frothy head—merely a few classy bubbles. The secret is to angle the flute and pour in just a little champagne—just over a centimeter or so should do for now. Wait a few seconds for the bubbles to disappear, then pour again until two-thirds of the glass is full. Drink holding the stem of the glass so as not to warm the champagne, chill the bottle in between pouring, and try not to belch.

Size matters

Champagne bottles come in more than one size:

Split or Piccolo (187.5 ml or 200 ml) – A quarter
   bottle, one for the ladies to suck through a straw

Demi (375 ml) – A cheeky half-bottle

Imperial (750 ml) – A standard bottle

Magnum (1.5 l) – 2 bottles in one

Jeroboam (3 l) – 4 bottles

Rehoboam (4.5 l) – 6 bottles

Methuselah (6 l) – 8 bottles

Salmanazar (9 l) – Just the 12

Balthazar (12 l) – 16 bottles

Nebuchadnezzar (15 l) – 20 bottles

Melchior (18 l) – 24 bottles

Solomon (25 l) – 33.3 bottles

Primat (27 l) – 36 bottles

Melchizedek (30 l) – 40 bottles, and you couldn't
   lift this fucker, let alone open and drink it.

How To...
Be The Perfect
Gentleman

The good news for all men is that you no longer need to be a total jackass to be a gentleman, unlike in the old days when it was all based on bank accounts. These days, a gent is nothing more than a courteous and honorable man.

He doesn't have to be from a "good family" and, luckily, there are so many macho idiots in society these days that even the occasional act of courtesy—particularly when directed toward a woman—will elevate you instantly above the maddening crowd.

Consider the following ten skills as mere stepping stones to a more gentlemanly existence. They are merely the basics; the mark of a true gent is that he's always keen to learn more. But space on the page is tight and, well, they're a start...

Rule 1. A true gent goes about his business with a minimum of fuss and drama. Nothing should surprise him or cause him to show dismay in public; not a run of bad luck at the track, nor the loss of his entire family in a bizarre yachting accident. Life's many tribulations cannot shake him from his stride.

Rule 2. A true gent never swears. His vocabulary should be sufficiently mature for him not to have to resort to the language of the gutter. Even when the talk around him is turning blue, he never lowers himself to such levels. However, if he does have to say 'shit' or 'fuck' for any reason, he'll first check over both shoulders to make sure no ladies are within earshot.

Rule 3. Only a vulgar man will be seen spitting on the floor. If he has to spit he should cough it up into a handkerchief—without making that big, guttural, phlegmy sound—and dispose of it later. Similarly, a man should never be seen rummaging a finger up his nostril, let alone waving his dirty catch around for all to see. Use a handkerchief, and don't give the contents more than a cursory glance.

Rule 4. A gentleman must walk like a gentleman: upright with his head held high. Never shuffle along dragging your knuckles and feet, nor swagger like a Broadway dancer. Aim for something in between and you should be safe.

Rule 5. A true gent knows how to conduct himself around women. He's punctual and polite. He stands when she enters the room, offers her his seat and helps her with her coat or the door. He maintains eye contact, laughs politely at her jokes, and treats her as an equal, even when buying her drinks all night or carrying a box that she claims is too heavy for her skinny frame. She may just be being lazy, but a gent would know better than to fling around accusations.

Rule 6. A gent also knows how to behave in mixed company at the dinner table. The list of etiquette is too lengthy to cover here, but let's just say that elbows should be kept off the table, talking with a full mouth is generally frowned upon, and soup should be sipped and not slurped. Also, if a gent discovers a hair in his food while dining, he does the gentlemanly thing and places it beneath the edge of his plate with the minimum of fuss, rather than accusing the chef of sticking his privates in the soufflé again.

Rule 7. A gentleman never ever laughs at the misfortunes of others, unless he happens to see a man hit in the privates with a baseball bat/golf club/hockey stick on TV. Then he can laugh heartily to confirm his well-rounded sense of humor.

Rule 8. A gentleman never carries a watch—he can always ask his servants if he needs to know the time. You can consider this one optional.

Rule 9. A gentleman never invites a woman to pull his finger. This one's *not* optional.

Rule 10. And a gentleman is never unconsciously rude or disagreeable. When he is rude or disagreeable, it's because he means to be—and on these occasions he's allowed to say 'shit' and 'fuck' all he likes.

How To...
Tackle A Thief

Get this right and there's probably a measly reward from the store owner for putting your life on the line. If the thief's making it easy for you, he'll be the one in the black-and-white sweater carrying the bag with the giant dollar signs. You'll need to bring the brute down and sit on him until the cops finally turn up, but how you stop him depends on which direction you're tackling him from...

Tackle from the front

If the thief's been stupid enough to run toward you with his head held high and his chest exposed, your job's much easier. You'll want to wind him by nail-ing him in the stomach with your shoulder as hard as you can. As your shoulder makes contact with his gut, drive through with your legs to maximize the impact and sit on him while he struggles to recover. If his head is down and his chest less exposed, aim to stick

your shoulder between his hip and abdomen, grab the backs of his legs and lift with a straight back to dump him on his ass. Or you could just opt for the safer option by allowing him to run past you before tackling him from the back.

Tackle from the back

The safest option of all. Approaching from the rear, focus on the back of the thief's thighs and get as close to him as possible. When in range, make contact with your shoulder on his thigh and position your head to one side of his leg. Straighten your back and wrap both arms around him. The combined momentum should see you slide down his legs and bring him to the floor, provided you manage to hang on for dear life.

Important disclaimer: Many thieves can be quite bad-tempered if you bother them while they're working. Attempt this trick at your own discretion—and don't come crying to us if the thief bashes your head in.

How To...
Blow A Smoke Ring

Society may look down its nose at cigarette smokers these days, but the man who can fire smoke rings effortlessly while puffing on a cigar remains the first name on any guest list. And rightly so: this guy's a suave entertainer who thumbs his nose at cancer just to keep you amused...

Your weapon of choice

If you want to be that man, you'll need a fat cigar. Although smoke rings can be achieved using a standard cigarette, it'll make you look like a poser or a cheapskate. Pipes produce enough smoke for a good ring, but they're reserved for weird uncles and social inadequates. So a good Cuban cigar works best.

The basic

Suck up a generous mouthful of smoke, but don't inhale or the trick will fall flat on its ass. You'll need to purse your lips as if you're about to say the letter 'O'. The size of that 'O' determines the size of the smoke ring—start small and build up. As you tighten your throat muscles, the underside of your tongue needs to flick the smoke out as a small puff of air–tongue control is everything here and you'll cough and splutter before you've mastered the art.

Getting the volume of smoke right is key—too little smoke and people will think you've merely coughed; too much smoke and they'll move away to someone less carcinogenic.

Trick puffs

With practice comes the ability to entertain entire dinner parties with your pollution. You've learned that the size of the 'O' determines the size of the ring, and trial and error will teach you how the duration and velocity of the exhalation controls the speed, while flexing your throat muscles allows you to shoot off rapid-fire rings.

Larger rings move more slowly through the air, which allows you the time to pull off the easiest piece of smoke-ring showmanship. Using the basic technique, send a large ring out into the air, then fire a smaller, faster-moving ring through its centre. Get it right and you'll prove once and for all that smoking actually is big and clever.

How To...
Pull Off The
Heimlich Maneuver

If there's one thing guaranteed to ruin a pleasant meal with lively company, it's noticing that one of your fellow diners is choking to death on their appetizer. The telltale signs are that they've turned a worrying shade of blue and started grasping their throat and gasping for air. These symptoms suggest that their windpipe has become blocked, and without assistance they'll surely die. Needn't panic though, for the trusty Heimlich Maneuver should save them.

First, encourage the victim to cough—that in itself could be enough to dislodge the object. If they can't cough, slap them on the back sharply five times, then check their mouth to see if the object has dislodged. If not, have someone call an ambulance (that part is important) as you perform the Heimlich...

Step 1. Wrap your arms around the ailing person's waist. Now, make a fist and place the thumb-side of it against the choker's upper abdomen, i.e., below the ribcage and above the navel. Tell your fellow diners not to panic, that you know what you're doing, you've done this sort of thing before, and so on and so forth. Keeping everyone calm is very important.

Step 2. Next, grasp your fist with your spare hand and press into their upper abdomen with a quick upward thrust. Squeezing the ribcage with your arms could inflict damage, so confine the force of the thrust to your hands.

Step 3. If you're lucky, there will be no Step 3: whatever was blocking the windpipe should at this point pop back out of their mouth. If it does, don't eat it. If it doesn't, repeat Step 2 until the object is expelled. Suggest to the victim that if they doubt the object has been completely removed they should proceed directly to a doctor, then let the waiter know that you have no intention of paying the bill.

The good doctor

Since its introduction in 1974, Dr. Henry J. Heimlich's trusty maneuver has saved more than 50,000 people, including the likes of celebrity chokers Ronald Reagan, Liz Taylor, and Princess Leia, or at least the woman who played her. Also, it can and has been used to save numerous pets who've been choking on nuts and dog biscuits and the like. Opinions as to its effectiveness vary across the world—it's banned in several countries, including Australia, due to the risk of injury even when performed correctly—but the Heimlich is generally considered the safest way of saving a choking victim.

How To...
Catch A Fish With A
Piece Of String

In theory, with enough training from bearded men who survive in the wilderness and live off the land, you could easily make a fishing line from numerous plant and bark shards, just as your ancestors did. Attach a bone sharpened into a dangerous point and you'd have yourself a makeshift hook with which you could snare fish all day long. Alas, there's no room on this page for all that, so let's agree that you're sitting by a river feeling foolish, armed with nothing more than a line of string and a can-do attitude.

There are hundreds of species of freshwater fish, many of which taste good with tartar sauce and French fries. One of the tastiest, the trout, loiters lazily in well-oxygenated freshwater rivers, and can be caught using the following technique.

Step 1. Hang around close to the river bank, in a position where you can observe what's going on beneath the water. Sunglasses with polarized lenses, which cut the surface glare, make it easier to spot a fish. Did you pack your sunglasses? Of course not. Then ignore that part and concentrate on keeping low to reduce your profile against the sky—if the fish spots you he's guaranteed to flee. You'll need to draw him towards you with tasty bait—earthworms and flies remain popular among fish. Take your bait and insert a line of fine thread through its body, using the pocketknife we're sure you packed. Then run the line through a small thorn that will act as a makeshift hook, and tie it all securely in place with a large knot at the end. Drop the line into the water and wait, making sure your shadow doesn't fall across the water and spook the fish.

Step 2. And wait.

Step 3. And be prepared to wait some more—stealth and patience are key here.

Finally, when a hungry fish takes the bait, the thorn should lodge in its throat or mouth. As he panics and you feel your line tighten, pull him on to the bank.

An alternative approach

If your line is particularly tough and sinewy, you could hunt eel rather than trout. Back in the olden days, fishermen would attach a gaggle of worms to the end of a line and wait for the eel to take the bait. Those fine fibers on the line would attach very easily to the eel's teeth, and no amount of wriggling would save him from the fisherman's clutches.

Another alternative

If you only have a length of thread or fine string and no bait, you could always tie it into a simple slipknot noose, drop it into the water and wait for the fish to float towards you. Without bait, this should take even longer than normal and you may fall asleep before you even see a fish. But if a fish is unlucky enough to float within range, gently maneuver the noose onto its tail or around the gills, tighten abruptly, and haul it out onto the river bank. This method is apparently also good for snaring small birds, but they don't taste quite as nice.

Tickling trout

Legend has it that if you wait long enough in a river a trout will present itself and allow you to tickle its belly. Then, after a couple of minutes, the tickling will send the trout into a blissful doze, at which point you lift him straight out the river and into a deep fryer. Sadly, the truth is less impressive. To catch trout by hand, you'll need to skulk about on the bank of a shallow, fast-flowing river or stream.* Feel gently around the stones and rocks, where trout like to loiter, until you touch something slimy–this should be the fish you've been looking for. Act fast to grip firmly around the underbelly and whip the fish out onto the bank before he can dart off downstream. Once he's on dry land, you can tickle him all you want.

This assumes you've paid for a legitimate permit to fish on the waters in question. It's illegal, otherwise.

How To...
Save A Drowning Person

You'll need to think fast here, although not so fast that you don't first consider the dangers involved to you, the would-be hero. Your natural instinct may be to dive head-first into the water and drag the thrashing drowner to safety, but you'd be a tad premature and endangering your own life...

Warning: Only ever enter the water as a last resort

If there's a stick or pole to hand, hold it out and suggest that the swimmer (well, drowner) hangs on as you haul him back to safety. If someone's thoughtfully hung a life ring on the end of a rope nearby, toss that instead and haul him back to dry land. Either way, make sure you're secure on the sidelines as you pull, so as not to get yanked in yourself. Finally, if there happens to be a boat on-hand, row out to the victim before employing the stick or ring methods.

If this stretch of water is lacking long sticks, floating rings, and useful boats, the only option is to enter the water—**But Only If You're A Trained Lifeguard**. If you're not, you've officially done all you can for this person and should now call 911 for assistance and wait. Unless you're trained, you should under no circumstances enter the water, even if the drowning person is a member of your family or a close friend who owes you money.

The danger is that in their blind panic, drowning people often drag their rescuer under the water as they struggle, very selfishly putting two lives at risk. A trained lifeguard would know that it's vital to talk to the victim as he approaches and to tell him he's about to help him back to shore. That would calm him down and allow the rescuer to hook his arm over the victim's chest from behind. He could then tell him to relax and float on his back to make things easier, as he used his free arm to sidestroke them both back to safety.

If the victim does drag this trained hero down, he'd know to swim down further under the water, aware that the victim will fight to return to the surface and thus set him free. Once back on shore, the expert would know to check the victim's airway, breathing and circulation, and how to administer CPR, if required (which he may have learned on pages 142–4). He'd also know to treat them with extreme care throughout so as not to exacerbate any injuries already sustained.

That's what he'd do. You, of course, are not trained so should stand helplessly on the river bank and watch as the victim disappears under the water.

Warning: this is based on relatively still waters rather than any stretch with dangerous undercurrents. Diving into the water is a risky business and you could lose your life. Man Skills *cannot recommend it, although a good lawyer will notice that we have already repeatedly advised against entering the water if you don't know what you're doing.*

How To...
Toss A Caber

Cabers have been thrown across fields by hairy brutes for centuries, often in warfare, when large logs were tossed into enemy battlements, or as a practical solution to logistical problems—logs were often chucked across rivers as makeshift bridges. Only in more recent times have cabers been tossed by men in skirts for the sheer unadulterated fun of it all.

Measure up
The professionals typically toss a 20-foot-long caber weighing between 80 and 135 pounds—which is almost certainly out of your league. Unless you want to hurt yourself, use a scaled-down version—which is shorter and lighter, and therefore easier to control. First though, consider the following…

Distance is irrelevant
Caber tossing is judged on technique and landing. To score high you'll need the caber to turn 180 degrees (end over end) in the air, land on what started out as the top end and fall directly away from you at what the professionals call the 12 o'clock

position. In competition, 12:00 rules, but 11:00 scores higher than 9:00, just as 1:00 is better than 3:00. If the caber lands on its end and falls back toward you, run for cover and expect to be marked down accordingly—forward falls always score higher than those that drop backwards. But we're getting ahead of ourselves here, because first you'll need to master the technique.

The technique

Assume the correct manly posture: heels together, toes out, the narrow end of the caber lying flat on the ground between your feet and facing away from you, mild fear etched across your face. The far end of the caber will be lifted off the floor and walked up towards you and into an upright position, so that it's now staring you straight in the face. At this point, it's probably too late to back out.

Step 1. Seasoned professionals will have coated their hands in tacky, a resin-and-turpentine mix that feels like molasses and keeps their mitts securely on the caber. Without tacky, your fingers will almost certainly be driven apart and the caber will fall on your foot.

Step 2. So, lock your sticky fingers together, bend at the knees and grip the caber. Get as much of your palms as possible around its base, dig both hands in firmly and stand up. Do it slowly and use your leg muscles rather than your arms to lift. The caber should come up easily enough, but then it gets tricky.

Step 3. The caber is now vertical and resting against your stronger shoulder, but half the battle is steadying the thing. You can expect to spend several minutes staggering around like a drunkard before you have it under full control, and only then are you finally ready to launch it.

Step 4. The technique can vary. Some people take a long run up, others just a few steps—do whatever feels most comfortable to you. With either approach, as you move forward, try to run the final few steps to gain momentum. As you approach the line, push the caber forward with your shoulder until it reaches a suitable launching angle (at least 45 degrees, at most 75), then drive your hands and arms forwards and upwards to create as much thrust as possible.

Now, stand back and watch it arc off into the distance, or run for cover and scream like a child as it drops back toward your head.

A load of old toss
For all you etymology fans out there, you might like to know that the word 'caber' comes from the early-sixteenth-century Scots Gaelic word *cabar*, meaning 'pole'. Or you might not. But it's too late now.

Tossers beware!

To attempt this skill, seasoned tossers warn that you'll need to be in 'good physical shape,' otherwise you're likely to pull or otherwise mangle something painful. Consult a gym instructor or trainer for a definition of 'good physical shape,' and mention to him that you'll need to work on your leg strength as that's where much of your tossing power will come from.

How To...
Deliver A Baby In An Emergency

First things first, a legal warning to consider before attempting this one: it's unlawful for anyone other than a registered midwife or doctor to plan to deliver a baby for other people. If you attempt to set up a lucrative business based on what you learn from this entry, you should expect a knock on the door from the cops followed by a large fine or a stretch in the big house.

This entry is for Times of Emergency Only, and you'll probably never have to call upon the wisdom it imparts. If you do, fret not, for your job can be summarized as a simple Catch and Dry operation. Hospital births have become a matter of custom rather than a matter of need only in the last hundred years or so. Before then, women were dropping newborns in fields, cowsheds, and ditches full of dung with little trouble. The point here is that labor is a natural event, not something to fear.

So, the method

There's no time to get the expectant mother to hospital, so you'll have to birth him (could be a her, but we're saying him) yourself.

Step 1. Luckily, babies do much of the work themselves, so you just need to be on hand to coax, cajole, and calm the mother down when she gets flustered. Keep telling her everything will be fine, she's in safe hands, you've read about it in that book she bought you for Christmas. Then call your doctor or midwife, then an ambulance—in that order.

Step 2. Make sure she's in a comfortable position on her hands and knees, close to the floor and forward-leaning so that the baby can traverse the pelvis in a natural way. Despite what you've seen on *ER*, she shouldn't be on her back on a bed. That's for the benefit of the doctor so he can see more clearly—plus the sight of a woman giving birth with her backside in the air is not so TV-friendly.

Don't encourage her to push. Women are generally very adept at delivering babies and their bodies will tell them when and how to breathe. Barking instructions like some drill sergeant may make you feel better about your minimal contribution, but it's helping nobody.

Step 3. Check to see if the baby's head is visible. If not, continue as you were, encouraging, glancing occasionally at your watch, and wondering what's taking that midwife so long.

If his head is visible, inform the mother, wait for the shoulders to emerge and then support the head in your hands and guide him gently towards the floor. Don't yank him out, you impatient oaf, he'll come out soon enough.

Step 4. The minute babies hit cold air, 99 percent of them take a deep breath and begin to wail.

If they don't begin breathing, they'll need mild resuscitation, which sounds more dramatic than it is. Simply take a towel and gently dry him off, working from the head down, taking special care around the soft spot on the top of the head (the fontanelle). Toweling warms and stimulates the baby, at which point he'll take a breath in and open his lungs loudly in your ear.

Step 5. More perceptive men may notice that the baby is still attached to the mother by the umbilical cord. This can remain attached safely for several weeks if need be, so there's no rush to cut it, particularly as you don't know what you're doing. Leave it for the midwife, because she does.

Step 6. Finally, wrap the baby in a dry towel and pass him to his mother, who should by now be sweaty, glowing, and teary-eyed. Shrug it off like it was no problem, then toast the baby boy with a stiff drink.

How To...
Hold A Baby
Properly

By properly, we mean without dropping it on its delicate little head or allowing its neck to loll painfully to the side.

The good news is that babies come with a clever built-in alarm that can help you gauge when you're holding them just right. The bad news is that until you get it right that alarm will scream until your ears drip blood.

The fact of the matter is that there's no right or wrong way to hold a baby, and no expert technique that only mothers know. It's simply trial and error, shuffling the baby around until he's comfortable—at which point he'll stop bawling and begin drooling on your shirt. That said, to avoid being patronized by any woman observing your ham-fisted attempts, memorize this idiot-proof technique.

With the baby in a lying position, scoop him up and hold his front against your chest, with his head turned to one side. Use one hand and forearm to support his bottom and take the weight, and the other to fully support his back, neck, and head.

The single undisputable law of Baby Holding is that you have to fully support his body, particularly the head and neck, because he doesn't yet have the strength or control to do it himself.

The key to any good hold is that you both need to be comfortable, but his comfort is far more important than yours and he's likely to scream until he vomits if you don't get it right.

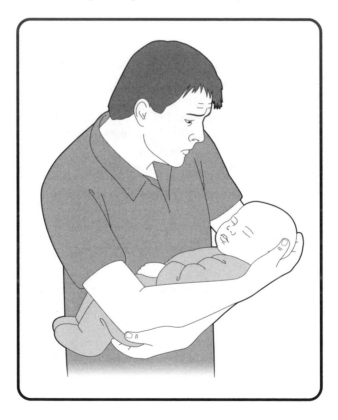

As this man recognizes, the most important thing is to provide support to the baby's head.

How To...
Pass Yourself Off
As Some Kind Of
Wine Buff

By 'wine buff' we mean the type of man who can order a half-decent bottle in a restaurant without coming across as a cocky old snob. Whether it's a first date, an important lunch with people in suits, or an attempt to win over suspicious in-laws whom you suspect might think you're hapless, stick to these ten basic rules and you won't go wrong. Or, at least, not too far wrong…

Basic Rules
1. Never ask the wine waiter to recommend a wine. How do you know for sure that he knows what he's talking about? And if he works on commission, what's to stop him from steering you towards a more expensive bottle? Do it yourself.

2. Don't let him pressure you into choosing. If you feel rushed in any way, simply make eye contact, project confidence, and say, 'Thank you, we'll decide shortly.' Never be pushed into choosing a wine you're unsure of or anything out of your price range.

3. Look for grape varieties and countries. Wily wine producers stick different labels on restaurant wine so you don't notice that you're ordering the same bottle you can get for $5 in a supermarket. Remember which grape varieties and countries you normally like, rather than the pretty sticker on the front, so that you recognize the name of a favorite vino when you spot it on a restaurant wine list.

4. With white wines, the younger the better. As a basic rule, whites are best aged a couple of years; any older and they'll almost certainly have lost a little of their fruity zing. With reds you can go a year further back, as they age slightly better. Cheaper wines diminish with age, expensive wines improve—you remember that.

5. Cheap doesn't always mean inferior. It's often merely less fashionable. A South African sauvignon is far cheaper than one from New Zealand simply because it's less 'fashionable,' though both taste equally good. Italian and Spanish grapes are also worth considering for the same reason.

6. With fish dishes of any kind…you're safe with all whites and most of the cheaper end of the New World reds—those from Argentina, Australia and New Zealand, for example. But with reds, avoid anything containing tannin as it will taste metallic with the fish and you'll screw your face up as you eat.

7. Overchilling white wine paralyzes the taste. You can tell if it's too cold if the glass frosts up when it's poured. To remedy this, ask the wine waiter to remove the bottle from the ice bucket or cooler and shove it up hi...er, and wait until it's warmed up before drinking. For this reason alone, wine should always be tasted before you eat (see below). If the food turns up before the wine, send it straight back with a contemptuous glare.

8. Never order wine without tasting it first. Make sure the bottle's opened in front of you to ensure it's the one you ordered. If the waiter opens the wrong bottle in front of you, it's your mistake rather than his. And if you don't like the taste of the wine you're trying but there's nothing actually wrong with it, you've chosen poorly and are expected to buy the bottle and learn from your mistake.

9. Send bad wine back. If a wine tastes oxidized (it'll be old, brown, and particularly dull-tasting) or if it's corked (it smells musty and moldy), send it straight back. Corked wine especially is still such a problem that you'll get one sooner or later and you won't be able to tell until the bottle's opened. Screw caps are replacing corks on many mid-priced wines, which helps, but even screw-cap wines need to be offered for slurping first as the wine may have been contaminated along the production line.

10. Buy champagne. If your only reason for ordering wine is to impress a date, buy champagne instead.

Yes, sparkling wine from New Zealand is a lot cheaper, often better and made in exactly the same way, but nothing has quite the same effect on shallow ladies as a bottle of over-priced champagne (see page 61, How To...Open Champagne (The Sophisticated, Unflustered Way)).

How To...
Pull Off A Handbrake Turn

For those occasions when a gentle three-point-turn just won't suffice, you might want to unleash your inner stuntman by pulling a quick handbrake turn instead. It's fairly easy to master...

You'll need:

- A suitable car, preferably a front-wheel-drive model with a 'lever and button-release' style handbrake. If the handbrake operates on the front wheels, find another car.
- A large open space—ideally a quiet, non-residential-type area where you won't get arrested. A damp or gravel surface will make it easier to pull off the turn and is less wearing on your tires, although that shouldn't concern a daredevil like you.
- A crowd of people drinking the cheap beer of their choice, several of whom are wearing hoods and spitting indiscriminately. Otherwise, if nobody else witnesses your U-turn, what's the point of doing it?

You'll need to cruise along at a leisurely speed of around 30 to 35 mph—any slower and you'd struggle to complete the 180 degrees, any faster and your momentum could end up taking you backwards—which looks uncool.

You should be in second gear at this point, with your dominant hand positioned so that it can give the wheel a full turn. The exact position depends on which way you want to turn: if you're turning the front end to the right, place your right hand on the left side of the wheel, at around the 7 o'clock position. If the car's going to the left, place the left hand on the right of the wheel, around the 5 o'clock mark. You're now about ready to pull your stunt, so this is how it should break down:

Step 1. Grip the handbrake and keep the release button firmly pressed in, but don't pull it up quite yet.

Step 2. Let your foot come off the accelerator, then step on the clutch (and keep it floored until the car stops).

Step 3. Sharply turn the steering wheel, at least a half-turn in your chosen direction. Speed is of the essence, so make it a good sharp tug.

Step 4. A mere fraction of a second after turning the wheel, pull up the handbrake and you should feel the car's rear brakes lock the wheels, and then the rear end start to move/slide in a 'controlled oversteer.'

Step 5. At this point you and your car should be rotating, which is when you need to counter-steer the wheel back to a neutral position. Do it gradually so you end up with all four wheels pointing straight when you complete the turn.

You'll need to experiment with the moment at which you release the handbrake—depress too quickly and you won't complete the turn, hold on too long and you'll over-cook it. Complex stuff such as vehicle weight, speed/velocity, and road surface/conditions dictate this, which is another way of saying you'll have to work out the release point for yourself.

Step 6. Apply the footbrake if you think the car will end up moving backwards. If everything's gone according to plan, you should now be facing the opposite direction. If the car's upside down, on its side, or just not fully turned, decide if you can be bothered to try again.

How To...
Break Down A
Locked Door

Before the cops take an active interest in this one,
let's emphasize that you're breaking down the door
in an emergency. There's a raging fire and you need
to escape, or you fear that whoever's on the other
side of the door requires some urgent medical attention, that kind of thing.

Under no circumstances should this skill be used
for burglary, partly because that's illegal and partly
because the technique you're about to learn
involves planting your foot through the door as
hard as you can, which would wake up every person in the street. If you're a burglar, you'd probably
be better off waiting till after dark and then picking
the lock.

The technique

A TV detective would run at the door, make contact
with his shoulder and be through in no time, even if
he was the type of flabby cop who gets out of breath
walking up stairs. Now, clearly that technique can
work, but only if you're a trained professional. For
the amateur, the chances of you dislocating your
shoulder are high and your momentum will carry

you through the door and into the room—and if there's a fire on the other side, you could well stumble right into the flames and burn to a crisp.

The safer technique is to put your foot through the door's weak point, which is to the side of where the lock is mounted—the keyhole gives it away. With as much force as you can muster, you'll need to land a firm kick to the lock area. Kick just to the side of the lock rather than directly on it, unless you want to break your foot.

Plant the underside of your foot as firmly as you can, using what can best be described as a half-assed karate kick approach. Make firm contact, push hard through the bottom of your foot and the wood should quickly splinter and the door fall open. If it doesn't, kick it again. And again. And again, if need be, particularly if it's a more sturdy exterior door. Eventually you'll get through, and danger will be averted.

How To...
Tie A Windsor Knot

In formal situations—interviews, court appearances, and particularly at weddings—a messy knot will mark you as an undignified ruin of a man, the kind of character who'll end the night drinking wine from his shoe.

The fat Windsor knot, by contrast, is the choice of the debonair; the type of knot that purrs supreme confidence. It is, according to fictional ladies' man James Bond, 'the mark of a cad,' which we're taking to be a good thing.

Now, if you're quite ready, flip the collar of your shirt up and begin...

Step 1. The fat end should extend about 30 cm below the thin end, hanging to your left as you look down. Cross the fat end over the thin and bring up through the loop between the collar and your tie; then feed it back down.

Step 2. Pull right so the fat end passes over your left index finger (which is holding the beginning of the knot in place), bring back behind the hand and up to the left, so the underside of the tie is now facing front.

Step 3. Bring the fat end across the front and to the right again, and at this point it should hook over the second finger on your left hand. Bring it under and up through the loop, then down through the by-now almost-formed knot in front.

Step 4. Tighten carefully and draw up to the collar, making sure it's not lopsided. Flip the collar back down, apply a splash of cologne, and enjoy your textbook knot in the mirror for a few moments.

Some rules, but by no means a definitive list:

The Windsor works best with light fabrics such as silk (rather than heavy woolen ties that will make the knot sag), and on wide-collared shirts where the knot can stretch out and breathe.

As a general rule, your tie should be darker than your shirt. If in doubt, look in the mirror and ask yourself a few searching questions.

A tie should hang just far enough to touch the waist on your slacks, which should be pulled up properly and not hanging around your ass like some punk teen.

When it comes to removing the tie, reverse the four steps above to keep it in pristine condition. Rip it loose as fast as possible and you'll distort its shape.

How To...
Buy A Used Car

Now, no one's claiming that all used car salesmen are confidence tricksters looking to swindle you out of your hard-earned savings, but there are always a few shysters who ruin it for the rest of them. Many used car salesmen are a credit to their profession; their vehicles are reliable, and comfortable, and represent incredible value for the money. They are a great bunch of guys. The others are scumbags, hence this guide.

This is by no means the definitive list, because buying a used car is a potential minefield of problems, but you'd be well advised to follow these lessons carefully before you consider swapping a large wad of cash for any set of keys.

Lesson 1. Do your homework

Before you go anywhere near a used car, scour magazines and websites for information on the model(s) you have in mind. You'll have a better idea of what's included as standard, the going price for your chosen model, and any potential problems you may encounter with this type of car.

Lesson 2. Shop around

Once you've narrowed it down to a particular model, shop around to get the best price. Search through car-trade magazine *Auto Trader* (www.autotrader.com) and the local papers, and then visit several local dealers.

Lesson 3. Play detective

Once you've located the ideal car to suit your taste and budget, investigate it further. Make sure it has a full service history, plus receipts to back it up. Read through the previous receipts—this will show you any problems the car's had, as well as giving you an opportunity to make sure that they've been rectified. If the car has been properly taken care of, the owner will be proud to show you the paperwork. If he doesn't have the records and he makes a crappy excuse for why not, make your own excuses and leave.

Lesson 4. Look closely

Only ever view a used car outdoors, in daylight, and in dry weather—rain can hide many defects in the paint job. Stand about 15 feet away and look for any changes in panel color, a sure sign of any previous accident damage. Every panel should be the same shade—any drips or blemishes suggest that it's recently been repainted. For the same reason, make sure the gaps between all panels look equal and flush. Uneven gaps between panels suggest they've been bolted back together after a crash. Excess paint around the windows and under the wheel arches should set warning bells ringing, as should fresh paint marks on the trunk or under the hood. How come you hadn't noticed the salesman's shifty eyes before now?

Lesson 5. Tread carefully

Check the tires for uneven wear—it's often a sign that the steering and suspension are damaged and need adjusting—at your expense. A new tire comes with 8 mm tread depth, and the legal limit is 1.6 mm. Any less than that and you're breaking the law and inviting mishaps. A tread-depth gauge will cost you next to nothing and take an accurate reading.

Also, as a basic but generally reliable test, check to see if the tires are all made by the same manufacturer. An owner who cares for his car will normally stick to the same brand.

Lesson 6. Drive on

Take the car out for a thorough test drive, perhaps packing a picnic and making a day of it through a nice country park. Once around the block will tell you jack about this motor—to give it a full road-test and check out its suspension and handling you'll need to be out for at least fifteen minutes driving on highways, country roads, through the city, and on bumpy surfaces. Listen for any unusual engine noise, rattles, and knocks, and push every button to make sure they are all in full working order. After the drive, check under the engine for any leaks or steam, and sniff for the ominous stench of burning.

Lesson 7. Call for help

If you're buying privately or without a warranty, have a mechanic inspect the vehicle for you. These men are trained, they know what to look for and, for a relatively minimal fee, they'll give you a detailed report and fewer sleepless nights. If they find something wrong that can be easily fixed, barter with the salesman to get some money off.

Lesson 8. Call for help again

According to some figures, as many as one in every twelve cars has been clocked—their mileage illegally altered by a scumbag in overalls. To check a car's previous form, including any insurance claims and its true current value, get a report on the vehicle's history from the DMV, Carfax.com, or Autocheck.com. If you only do one thing on this list, make it this one.

Lesson 9. Buy local

Buying closer to home means you can return the car if there's a problem. If it's a dealer, he'll want to uphold his reputation, so selling you a faulty motor is not a wise move. If it's a private sale you have less legal comeback, so be suspicious to the point of paranoia. Shady dealers sometimes sell privately to evade legal responsibility, while unscrupulous individuals will do all they can to cover their tracks. Beware private traders with several cars for sale, advertisers with mobile contact only, and shifty individuals who give vague, evasive answers and twitch a lot. Only ever view at the seller's property so you know where to address any complaints. If he suggests meeting in a bar parking lot or some quiet country lane in the middle of nowhere, tell him to f*^% off.

Lesson 10. The golden rule

If in doubt about any aspect of the car, or the dealer, take your business elsewhere.

How To...
Unclog The Toilet

It really couldn't be any easier, which makes you wonder why a plumber will charge you $100 just to come out, scratch his chin, shake his head, and chirp: 'Dear oh deary me—stopped up, is it?' before prodding around the U-bend with a stick for an extra $50. You're far better off fixing it yourself. Like so...

How to fix it yourself

If the water level rises almost to the rim and then drains very slowly, there's probably a blockage in the section of pipes your waste is flushed along, or the drain it discharges into. It's most likely a mix of excess toilet paper and a large manly deposit.

Never flush the toilet over and over in the hope that the blockage will just disappear on its own. It won't—and you'll get filthy water all over your bathroom floor. Instead, you'll need to force the water down the toilet to dislodge the blockage.

For this you'll need a plunger to create the pressure. Before you begin, scoop out any high water into a bucket, then take said plunger and insert into the bottom of the bowl to block the outlet. Push down two or three times, firmly enough for a few splashes of murky toilet water to jump out. You're wearing a pair of long rubber gloves, so it won't matter, although it may smell slightly ripe.

If you have no plunger, a long-handled mop works fairly well. Failing that, a wire coat hanger unfurled can be poked down the toilet to probe round the bend. It's also said that a bread knife kept beside the toilet to cut up bulky waste also sorts the problem at source, but you should avoid using the knife to slice anything else thereafter.

When the blockage has been dispersed, the water level should drop to normal. Flush to see if it's cleared properly. If it rises high again, repeat the process.

If it still doesn't clear, accept defeat and begrudgingly call a plumber. It could be that you'll need to clear the underground drain, which would involve fishing around in feces. So why not let a plumber earn his money for once?

How To...
Put Yourself Out When You Catch On Fire

It's sadly inevitable that at some point in your life this will happen. One minute you're walking past a naked flame, the next you're ablaze and screaming 'Arggh, arggh, ooohh, arggh!' You'll need to act fast and think a little more calmly if you're to avoid becoming a huge fireball.

Flames need oxygen to survive, so running around is playing right into their fiery hands. You'll need to snuff the flames out by starving them of oxygen. The easiest way to do this is to jump into a river or have at least a dozen people simultaneously spit on you. Failing that, these three crucial steps could be your only hope...

Step 1. Stop running around screaming like a girl. Stay calm and still.

Step 2. Drop down onto your front. This helps prevent the flames from spreading upwards to your face and head, where they'll do some serious damage to your pretty-boy features.

Step 3. Finally, roll on the ground to snuff the flames out. Deprive them of oxygen and they'll quickly die out.

Of course, if you discover someone else on fire, ensure they follow the above procedure, then help snuff out the flames by patting them down with a blanket at Step 3.

Disclaimer: like most of the entries in this book that involve potentially dangerous or life-threatening situations, this advice is to be used in genuine emergencies only, and not to bail out anyone who's been set on fire as a prank.

How To...
Iron A Shirt

Job interview, wedding, funeral, hot date: there comes a time in every man's life when his appearance really matters, and when only a crease-free shirt will do. As with the rest of this book, we're working on the assumption that you can't get your mother or other half to do it for you, so here's all you need to know.

Preparation

First, check the label on your shirt so you know what material you're dealing with—some are more delicate than others, such as silk, although if you can afford to wear silk shirts you can afford to pay someone to wash, iron, and hang your entire collection of shirts. And, to avoid confusing men like you and me, most iron manufacturers include handy symbols on their products which match the symbols on your shirt and tell dolts like us exactly what to do. Matching them up should be a breeze; linen setting for a linen shirt, cotton for cotton, etc. for etc., and so on. For the best results, iron the shirt when it's slightly damp to avoid creases and wrinkles setting into the material.

Before you begin, test your iron on the inside of your shirt (on a section that won't be visible) to make sure it doesn't scorch an iron shape onto your garment. If you're doing more than one shirt, start with those which need a lower temperature and build up to the higher heat.

Ironing experts suggest that if you're working with a steam iron, distilled water is essential to avoid clogging the iron and leaving unsavory sedimentary deposits all down your shirt, which will undermine all your hard work. Now, working on the inside of the shirt, iron in the following order…

1. Collar and cuffs

Place the underside of the collar flat on the board and hold it taut to avoid wrinkles, then iron from the outer points towards the center—your best bet for avoiding creases. Repeat on the front of collar, then iron both sides of both cuffs.

2. Sleeves

Ensure the sleeve is flat on the board, elbow side first, and that the seam is aligned neatly at the sides. The seams are the most difficult part to iron, but if you ignore them you'll look like you just couldn't be bothered to do it properly. Work up from the bottom of the arm to the top. Repeat on the other arm, then iron the fronts of both arms in the same manner while allowing your mind to wander onto something more interesting. Like cheese.

3. Back

Position the shoulder over the narrow, pointy end of the board and iron towards the center, then repeat on the opposite shoulder. Now lay the back of the shirt flat on the board and iron out any creases in whatever style you see fit. Some experts suggest that moving left to right across the shirt produces the best results, others claim right to left, but they're just bickering for the sake of it and it really doesn't matter. The end result should be that you remove any and all creases.

4. Front

Finally, flip the shirt over and lay one side of the front flat on the board. This is the most vital side as it'll be on view to anyone who tries to talk to you, so even if you've rushed through stages 1, 2 and 3, take extra effort here. If the shirt has a pocket, start on that side and apply extra pressure around the button-holes and between the buttons—if your iron's any good, it will have grooves which allow you to maneuver easily around them. Repeat over any areas you missed or which still have creasing, then hang immediately or slip straight on—there are no hard or fast rules where this one's concerned. Just remember to turn off the iron, then to double-check it an hour later when doubts begin to creep in.

If in doubt, cheat

For the man who's too lazy to run an iron over his shirt, there is apparently another way, one which requires almost no effort at all. Before you clamber into the shower, hang the shirt just out of range of the water but close enough for the steam to penetrate its fibers. When the steam gets in, many of the creases will drop straight out (and onto the floor).

For even better results, albeit with a little more planning and effort needed on your part, put the shirt on a hanger and button it up. Turn the shirt upside down and attach a clip hanger at the bottom—a clip hanger being one of those with clip attachment things at the bottom. Hang said shirt close to the shower, as before, but weigh it down by threading a heavy towel through the clip hanger's triangle. The added weight will pull the shirt taut and the tension on the fibers should stretch the creases out. You may need to shower for upwards of an hour to get every last crease out, but if it saves you the bother of ironing then who's complaining?

How To ...
Dive Like Tarzan

The only problem here is that Tarzan had a penchant for diving head first off craggy cliff tops, which is far too dangerous to recommend to a novice. So, let's relocate to the swimming pool or the sea, and learn from the modern-day doyen of the dive: Mitch Buchanan of *Baywatch*.

Now, the 'Mitch Buchanan Hollywood Dive' is typically used to save drowning women in tight bikinis, with the hero dressed in nothing more than a pair of tight, nut-hugging swimming briefs. These are optional, but with your beer gut you'd probably be better off wearing something with a more generous cut. What's not optional, however, is that unless you're trained in the ways of lifesaving, the MBHD should only ever be used to inject a little showmanship into your pool or sea entry. It should unfold as follows...

The 'Mitch Buchanan Hollywood Dive'
Step 1. A smooth, controlled entry into the water is the key. Take a few steps as you run up, plant your weaker foot on the edge of the boat or side of the pool and push your body forward with your

stronger foot. Really drive through with the push to get enough distance on the dive and avoid a belly flop over the edge.

Step 2. Aim for a graceful 45-degree 'loop' up and down into the water, so that as your body dives forward, your arms should come together in front of you with both hands forming a 'V' position, thumbs locked into place. Your head should dip down comfortably, just far enough to give you a more streamlined entry into the water.

Step 3. As you dive, focus on a small square on the surface of the water. Your whole body needs to dive through that imaginary square, so it needs to remain as straight as possible throughout the dive. Your arms should be relaxed, but held with enough tension to keep them straight throughout.

Mitch would tell you that the square technique makes things easier as it keeps your body compact throughout and promotes a graceful arcing entry into the pool—rather than the bellyflop of a flabby, artless amateur. Listen to the man.

How To...
Spit-Shine Shoes
(So You Can See Your Face In Them)

Any idiot can shine a pair of shoes with polish and a brush, but only a select few have mastered the art of coughing up a thick glob of phlegm and buffing up a shoe so ferociously that it's like looking into a mirror, albeit a very black mirror designed to confuse. There's more than one good reason for that: it's unhygienic, it takes forever, and ultra-shiny shoes make you look like a girl. But even so, for any would-be soldiers, bankers, or male dancers who may be reading, here's how you achieve 'the look'...

Step 1. Apply a medium-thick layer of paste over your chosen shoe (sports shoes are ill-advised, particularly white ones). A standard black shoe polish from any supermarket will suffice, but a specialist polish with some reference to the military in its name gives better results. Let sit for five minutes while it dries.

Step 2. Wrap a soft, clean cloth around your index finger, stretched over so it's tight and smooth. Spit on it, applying enough saliva for the cloth to be wet but not dripping. You can use water, yes, but then how is that a spit-shine?

Step 3. Using a brisk, efficient circular motion, buff the dried polish until the wax starts to become nice and shiny. If it helps you work, imagine that an angry drill sergeant is barking orders into your face while calling your mother all manner of crude names, none of which are true. As far as you know.

Step 4. Still using the damp rag, apply a fine layer of polish in a circular motion until a hazy shine begins to appear. Keep building up the layers until you have a completely smooth surface, but on each application use less polish and less force so as not to rub away the layers beneath that you've already worked in.

Step 5. Repeat until you can finally see your grinning mug staring back, accepting that this could well take several hours, hours you will never get back and may one day later regret frittering away on something so trivial as shoe maintenance. Use a soft, clean cloth to give shoes one final buff, then move on to the next page.

How To...
Make A Baby Stop Crying

Change its diaper, put it to bed, feed it, pick it up, bounce it about aimlessly on your knee, put it down, insert pacifier, remove pacifier, sing to it, waggle a toy in its face, make odd gurgling noises, change its diaper again, or just hand it back to its mother, shake head in shame, and shuffle quietly to one side.

How To...
Use A Straight Razor

When it came to slashing customers' throats, popular nineteenth-century barber Sweeney Todd put his faith in the straight razor—one quick slash of the trusty blade and the unfortunates were ready to be turned into rancid pies by 'Mad' Marge Lovett, his hoary accomplice. The customers he didn't butcher left his shop after the closest shave of their life, and to this day whisker experts declare the straight razor to be the best a man can get. It remains highly dangerous, so approach with caution...

Before you begin

Rinse your face with hot water to soften your whiskers, open the pores, and ensure a closer shave. Lather the shaving area with shaving cream, preferably glycerine-based, using a circular motion with the bristles of the brush to lift the hairs and produce a rich, creamy lather. Experts suggest a badger-hair shaving brush works best, although badgers recommend a ferret-hair brush. Prepare the skin properly and the blade will glide across your face and give you a closer shave.

The shave

Step 1. Open the razor by gently gripping the handle with your thumb and three fingers. With the open handle pointing away from the face, place your little finger in the crook of the blade for a secure grip. The angle of the blade is determined by the contours of your face, but experts suggest you start at a 30-degree angle.

Step 2. Which part of your face you shave first is your call, but it's vital to hold the skin taut with your free hand—creating a flatter surface will help the blade glide more smoothly. As you shave, each stroke of the blade should follow the grain of your whiskers and run smoothly for 3 to 4 centimeters at a time.

Step 3. When you've shaved the whole beard, re-lather and start again. The smoothest shaves take two passes, but this time the strokes of the blade should run against the grain of the beard.

Step 4. After two shaves your face should be as smooth as the day you were born, but hopefully less bloody. Rinse with cold water and apply a moisturizing balm. In preparation for next time, rinse the razor thoroughly with hot water, wipe dry, and store out of the reach of children and demented barbers.

Bloody hell

For any minor nicks along the way, apply a moistened alum block to the cut. This magical soap-sized block possesses blood-vessel-constricting astringent properties to curb any minor blood loss. A styptic pencil does a similar job, and both are far more effective than plastering toilet paper all over your face.

How To...
Rip A Phone Book
In Half With Your
Bare Hands

Even if you're a 6-foot-3-inch stick figure with the strength of an arthritic old lady, you will be able to pull this one off. Your build is irrelevant (writes a 6-foot-3-inch stick figure with etc., etc.), as it's all down to a combination of technique and trickery. The trick is simply to break the spine*—once that's ripped, those flimsy pages will offer far less resistance.

The spineless approach
First, grip the book by its spine with both hands 3 to 4 centimeters apart. Your index fingers should be close together and along the top face of the book, with both thumbs along the bottom.

Bend the binding back and forth until it begins to tear, and then bend it back so the spine is straight again. Hold the book close to your body, around the stomach area and with your arms bent at 90 degrees –hold it at arms' length and it's far harder to gain the purchase and power needed to break through that spine.

Now, in one brisk movement, tear down the rip in the spine and through the pages, leaving two halves of a phone book. What you're going to do with two tattered halves of a phone book is not an issue right now.

A half-baked cheat's guide

If you need to weaken the spine further before attempting to rip through it, shove it in the oven at a very high temperature and bake for a few minutes until it crumbles slightly in your fingers. Allow to cool and the pages should be dry and brittle enough to rip through with little resistance. Nobody need ever know.

Professional phone-book rippers consider breaking the spine to be a cop-out option, as they tear through the pages first and finish at the spine. However, unless you have any ambition to turn professional, let's agree that they can shove their rules up their asses.

How To...
Make A Bow And Arrow

This entry is laboring under the notion that one day you'll be pitched into a big forest with nothing to survive on but your wits. However, it's far more likely that one day your son will ask you to whittle him a bow and arrow like a proper dad should, instead of showing him the six-month pre-record feature on your new DVD recorder. Either way, the following instructions should just about cover the basics...

Building a bow

Yew is traditionally the wood of choice, although in theory any old piece of wood will make a bow as long as it provides enough tension when you tighten the string. Find a six- (yes, six) foot pole or branch, preferably one that's not too green, and place one end on the ground.

Take a sharp implement, ideally an axe or another manly tool that will trim down the branch, and taper the stick from the center to the end—it should be thicker and sturdier in the center, and fat enough for your hand to grip firmly. Taper in the same fashion towards the other end, cutting nocks (small indents) for the string in both ends with a knife.

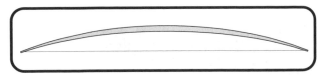

Take a length of string, attach it to both ends and tighten so the bow becomes taut and gives you a decent twang. Animal sinew, bark from certain trees, and even resilient nettles would also work, but string's much easier. You now have yourself a working bow.

Adding the arrows

Unlike the knobbly bow, your arrows have to be made accurately if they're to fly straight. You'll need a few lengths of reed or bamboo, and each piece needs to be as straight as possible.

Even then, the chances are that your crooked, would-be arrow won't be straight enough to use, so you'll need to hold it over a fire until the wood softens, allowing you to bend and straighten it by hand. Use your generic whittling tool to smooth it out as much as possible and to reduce its drag through the air. Now make several more, otherwise every time you fire your solitary arrow you'll need to chase after it and find it.

Cut a nock at one end and glue a small feather a couple of centimeters or so down the shaft to make the arrow fly straighter and look more professional. Finally, sharpen to a point at the other end so that when you fire it from the bow it will stick in all manner of woodland vermin. Just make sure you have all the necessary permits, know the guidelines, and, if you're with buddies, are dressed in orange. Arrows smart.

How To...
Fire A Bow And Arrow

Should you wish to fire a bow and arrow, perhaps using the one you made on the previous pages, try aiming at a big circular board or a tin can on a wall before you start shooting at animals (and hitting your aforementioned buddies), then set yourself up like so...

Step 1. Stand side-on to your target with your feet about shoulder's width apart and your toes facing forwards, but with the tips of your shoes forming an imaginary line down towards the center of the target.

Step 2. Place the notched end of the arrow on the string so it sits comfortably, and hold it in place so that the arrow rests between the index and middle fingers of your dominant hand.

Step 3. Hold the bow grip with your other hand and allow the far end of the arrow to rest on the top of the hand, just above the knuckle. Beginners might like to wear a glove for extra safety.

Step 4. Bring the bow arm up to shoulder height, and draw the string back in a straight, horizontal line, keeping both shoulders as low as possible and with your shoulder blades moving towards each other. Stay relaxed as you focus on the target.

Step 5. Pull the string as far back as the middle of your chin. Your index finger should rest beneath the chin. Your bow hand, your draw hand (the one pulling the string) and your elbow should form as straight a line as possible, with the back muscles remaining tense and both shoulders kept as low as possible. Keep the bow arm slightly bent out, away from the path of the string.

Step 6. Aim with the eye that's furthest from the target, and shut the other to focus. Keep the point of the arrow aimed at the target, elevating it slightly to compensate for distance—the further away the target, the higher you'll need to aim to compensate for the arrow losing height as it travels.

Step 7. Steady your body and the shot by closing your mouth, clamping your teeth together and holding your breath. Pull back the string—the further you pull the further it will fly, unless you pull too far and it snaps (in which case, turn back to the previous entry). Release the string and the arrow should, in theory, twang off towards the target.

Step 8. Keep aiming at the target until the arrow has struck. For extra artistry points and a more dramatic flourish, when you release the string your draw hand should be near or behind your ear.

Step 9. Now, with the next arrow, coat the head in paraffin, set fire to it, and launch it onto the nearest thatched roof.

Step 10. No, hold on. The Fun Police say you can't do that. Crap.

These instructions are based on firing a longbow only; other bows require different techniques. They're good for both left- and right-handed men, though.

How To...
Jump-Start A Car

You can swear at your car all you like, but *it* didn't leave the lights on overnight or while you were at work all day, so if anyone's an 'effing jackass' in this sorry episode, it's probably you.

But it doesn't matter, because having read this entry, you know the importance of carrying a set of jumper cables in your trunk. They're available from all half-decent car accessory shops and will resuscitate a drained battery in minutes. You also know better than to jump-start a frozen battery, of course, because it will explode. But that's another matter altogether.

As well as the jumper cables, you'll need a friend with a healthy car, or a stranger kind enough to let you bumble around under his hood and drain his battery for fifteen minutes. You'll need to check both cars' manuals to ensure the batteries are the same voltage and both jump-start-friendly, but you're not stupid and would have done that anyway so you're about ready...

Step 1. Position the good car next to the bad before switching off both ignitions and all electrical equipment. Apply both emergency brakes and put the cars into neutral (or P for automatics), and, to avoid an explosion, extinguish any cigarettes, pipes, or cigars before opening both hoods. The cars should be close enough to comfortably attach the cables, but never touching—unless you want to scratch the paintwork and risk sparks or a giant explosion. Which, yes, would be cool, but this is your car we're talking about.

Step 2. On the bad car (although we're not blaming him, it wasn't his fault), connect one end of the red jumper cable to the positive terminal on the battery, marked with an idiot-proof '+' sign. Attach the other end to the positive terminal on the good car's healthy battery, making sure that as you move the wire across it doesn't touch any metal on the vehicle, including (obviously) the bodywork.

Step 3. Now take the black jumper cable and connect one end to the negative ('−') terminal of the good battery and the other end to any unpainted metal surface under the hood on the bad vehicle, providing it's well away from the battery, fuel systems, carburetor, or any moving parts. Never connect this end to the negative terminal on the bad battery—it could be okay, or both batteries could explode. So just don't do it. Also, never touch negative and positive clamps together or you'll destroy both batteries. And beware of any small sparks flying, which may make you scream like a small child.

Step 4. Wait three minutes for the voltages to equalize before starting the good car up and letting it run for a minute or so, then start the bad car up and run both at a fast (but idle) speed for ten minutes. If you don't keep the cables connected throughout, you risk damaging the cars' electronics.

(If your engine still won't start, turn off the engine, readjust the red clamp by either reattaching or turning it for a better connection and start again. If it still fails, your problem may run deeper than a dead battery and you'll need to call out the expensive men in overalls.)

Step 5. Ten minutes later, turn off the ignition on both cars and disconnect the cables in reverse order. Be careful not to undo all your good work by touching the clips against each other, yourself, or the car's bodywork.

Step 6. If successful, restart your engine and flick on the lights, the rear defrost, and the heater to prevent any voltage surges. You'll need to keep your car running for at least half an hour to recharge the battery, whether you're revving away in a parking lot or tearing up the roads. When you do finally drive off, take great care not to stall. Also, be aware that draining your battery like that won't have increased it's lifespan—it may be prudent to drive straight to a garage to have it checked or replaced. That might teach you to turn your lights off.

How To...
Perform CPR

The Grim Reaper has his paws all over another victim and is working fast, so there's no time to stand around scratching your chin and deliberating possible remedies.

The victim has stopped breathing and appears to have no pulse. In this situation it's usually a cardiac arrest, most commonly caused by a heart attack, most commonly caused by doughnuts, cheese, and slothful ways. If the heart stops beating normally, oxygen can't be pumped around the body effectively. Without meaning to put a downer on the book, when that happens, damage to the brain occurs after four minutes, which becomes irreversible after seven minutes and permanent after fifteen. So look sharp...

CPR, the Kiss of Life
(or cardiopulmonary resuscitation)

If the victim is unresponsive, he won't react if you shout or poke him. To check, ask him loudly if he's OK...If he doesn't respond, you'll need to follow the most basic 'ABC' routine. Check that his airway ('A') is clear by tilting his head back and lifting his chin forward, then look in his mouth for any obstructions (including his own tongue). Check for breathing ('B') by looking and listening for any chest movement. Finally, check for indications of blood circulation ('C'), by feeling for any signs of a pulse— the wrists and neck are the easiest places to identify a pulse. The ABC procedure should take no more than ten seconds to perform and if there's no response, call an ambulance before beginning CPR, just in case worse comes to worst. The first few minutes are critical to help keep the key organs alive until the ambulance arrives or the victim begins to show clear signs of recovery. CPR for adults is a combination of chest compressions and rescue breaths. CPR for kids is detailed afterwards.

Step 1. Chest compressions

Lie the victim on his back, providing he can be safely moved into position without sustaining or aggravating an injury. With your hands placed in the middle of the chest, right between the nipples, and with one on top of the other, push down firmly to perform one chest compression.

Press down between 4 and 5 cm, aiming to pump at a rate of 100 compressions every minute, i.e. faster than one every second. This alone could revive the victim, though you might hear a sharp cracking sound. That's just his cartilage or ribs cracking, but when the alternative is death he can't really complain. If thirty chest compressions don't rouse him, prepare to give him two rescue breaths.

Step 2. Two rescue breaths

Tilt the head back to open the airway, then pinch the victim's nose, cover their mouth with yours and blow for a second, until you see the chest rise. Give another quick breath, again lasting only a second, then apply thirty more chest compressions.

If there is no reaction, repeat the procedure. If the breaths are successful, the victim will cough and splutter and may even show their appreciation by vomiting on you. Turn their head to the side so they don't choke, wipe away as much vomit as possible and continue with CPR, or see if someone else wants to take over from here. No takers? Continue until the person begins to breathe normally and the ambulance arrives carrying the experts who can finish the job. If you got the victim this far, you can feel very proud of yourself.

One for the kiddies

These instructions remain much the same for children and babies, apart from that you should begin with five rescue breaths, and then revert to cycles of thirty compressions and two breaths. Use only one hand (assuming he's smaller than you) to make the compressions, and just two fingers for a baby.

How To...
Build A Fire

When roaming the great outdoors in search of manly adventure and a few of life's big answers, you'll no doubt need to hunker down for the night, preferably around a roaring fire. The warmth could keep you alive if it's a particularly fridgid night, plus it also allows you to cook and eat any beasts you've caught during the day. Now that the needless scene-setting is taken care of, here's how to construct the world's simplest fire...

Burn, baby, burn

You'll need a fire that's quick and easy to assemble, and there's none more quick or easy than the Tepee Fire. As the name suggests, it's shaped like a tepee, and built to allow enough oxygen in to burn the fuel but also to protect the flames from the wind.

Begin by feeling the ground. If it's wet, scatter a bed of dry leaves and twigs to keep the fuel as dry as possible until the flames have been established. Then construct as follows...

Step 1. Place the dry tinder (dead grass, straw, wood shavings, feathers, anything small that will burn) in the center and build up a few small sticks of kindling (twigs and strips of wood, dry pine cones broken up into small pieces, or dry leaves) into a small tepee over the top. The kindling should be no smaller than a matchstick and no bigger than a pencil, positioned so there's enough space to insert your hand to light the fire and to allow it to breathe. Keep a supply of kindling on-hand to add onto the fire as it burns, keeping it as dry as possible for very obvious reasons.

Step 2. Unless you're lighting with two sticks (see page 13), strike a match and hold it downward for a moment to allow the flame to stabilize and burn. Touch the flame on the tinder and carefully place (never throw) extra kindling on top until the fire builds up nicely. As the tepee burns, the outer logs will fall inward, feeding the fire. Keep adding the smaller wood, then apply the bigger, bulkier pieces.

Step 3. If you run out of dry wood, dried grass twisted into bunches and dried animal dung burn very well indeed, and no man should leave home without the latter.

Safety issues

If you build a fire beneath long, overhanging branches or close to bushes, you could soon have a much larger fire on your hands than originally planned. Clear a patch of ground before you begin.

If the wind is whipping in and causing no end of troubles, dig down into the ground to create a sheltered fire pit. Use your hands and any sharp implements available to create a pit 1 foot deep by about 2 feet wide, then build your tepee at a lower, more protected level. Have a pile of soil on hand to snuff out the fire, just in case it spreads out of control, and clear up all that mess before you move on.

How To...
Stage-Dive

Aren't you a bit old for that?

How To...
Win An Arm-Wrestling Contest

Luckily, you don't need to be six feet tall and made of muscle to win an arm-wrestling match: speed, technique, and strategy are as vital as pure strength. The key is to hit your opponent so fast that by the time he's caught on to what just happened, you're showered, changed, and enjoying a celebratory drink at the bar.

Top-rolling is the simplest and most effective technique in arm-wrestling, providing you get it right. This method is not about the biceps and fore-arms, but rather a battle of hand, finger, and wrist strength. Your aim is to force intense pressure on your opponent's hand—this will 'open up' his grip and allow you to strengthen yours. Denied the power he needs, you're in position to go in for the kill and touch his arm down on the table. This is how the whole episode should, in theory, unfold...

The set-up

Make a fist in front of you, with the top of your thumb and the nail facing towards your nose—the thumb should about 20 cm away from your nose. The line from your shoulder to your elbow (essentially the bicep) should be behind your forearm—if it's in front, your arm is already heading backwards, towards inevitable defeat.

Look down at your index finger; the first two knuckles should be facing high towards the ceiling as you make the fist. If you imagine a horizontal line between those two knuckles, you'll be attempting to pull that line towards your nose. Despite what you may think, there's absolutely no sideways pushing in arm-wrestling. You should only be trying to maintain the position of your arm in its strength 'sweet spot' (the start position) and then pull backwards towards your body, as if pulling a glass of beer.

Your arm and body should remain in that optimum position and move as one unit. The arm will obviously move—preferably to the left as you close in on victory—but the angles of wrist and fingers need to remain in position throughout, otherwise you'll lose power and risk pulling a muscle.

The technique

With the top-roll, your aim is to beat your opponent by rolling his wrist backwards and his arm over. This is apparently simple enough.

When you hear the words 'Ready, Go,' you're off. Pull back your arm very smoothly. Never jerk the arm in an attempt to finish your opponent off quickly, as you're more likely to screw up that optimum position mentioned earlier. Force his arm towards you and away from his body and you disrupt his optimum position. Work fast to gain greater leverage and build on your advantage. If his grip loosens, try to walk your fingers out, re-grip higher up his hand and then work them out a little bit more. Keep going and you'll eventually have enough leverage to take him down.

A word of warning

In the unlikely event that he somehow gets the upper hand, make sure your shoulder and your whole body stay with your arm and move in the same direction. Don't ignore everything you've just learned and apply a desperate sideways yank of the arm. Keep the pressure consistent and chip away at his grip to turn the pressure back on him. If you retain your optimum position, dig deep into your reserves, and psyche him out with 'the evil eye,' you should have the upper hand.

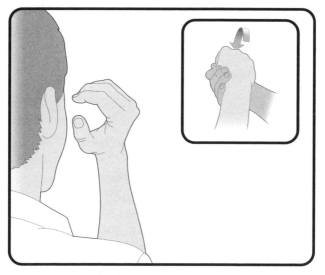

Main image: *The basic grip and set-up (opponent clearly not pictured).* Smaller image: *Re-grip high up to weaken your opponent's grip.*

How To...
Fend Off A
Dangerous Beast

Most animals you encounter during your lifetime will be of the cuddly or fluffy variety: kittens and ponies and little bunny rabbits with big floppy ears who want nothing more than to rub their little nose against yours. But what about the nasty bastard animals that prefer to bite, trample, and shred you to death? How do you escape unscathed when they attack? Luckily, this rough guide to surviving four of the most common psycho animal attacks might just save your ass...

A snappy, snarling dog

Now, not all dogs are bastards, but because you can never tell until one snaps and goes for your throat, it pays to approach them all with suspicion.

The golden rule is: never approach a strange dog, particularly not on its own turf and never if it's eating, sleeping, chewing anything, or surrounded by puppies. Most dogs will only bite as a last resort. They'll bark, growl, and puff out their chests as a way of defending their ground and telling you to move on, but it's usually no more than bravado.

If the hound keeps its distance or backs away from you, it views you as more dominant and knows better than to attack.

If it scampers over, its tail wagging and big, slobbery tongue hanging out, you should be safe enough. He only wants to lick your hand and sniff your privates. This one poses no threat.

If, however, it approaches all snarly, staring at you with its tail held high, he wants a piece of you. The worst thing you can do is turn on your heels and run, or even walk quickly away—a dog's natural instinct is to give chase.

Back off very slowly, facing the dog and showing no fear. Dogs can read fear in your eyes and your movement. They're also paranoid enough to feel threatened if you stare into their eyes, so avoid making eye contact. And if they catch you smiling at them, even nervously, a dog sees you baring your teeth and thinks you're looking for a rumble.

Stay calm, talk to the dog firmly, perhaps complementing it on its lovely glossy coat and powerful-looking teeth, and back away from it very slowly.

That might be enough, but if worse comes to worst and the dog attempts to snap his jaws down on you, you'll need to shove something in its mouth for it to bite on: a coat, umbrella, or suitcase would do; just anything that's not full of blood and attached to your body.

If you have nothing suitable to give him, feed him your arm, preferably wrapped in a thick sleeve to soften the pain. If the choice is between the arm or the dog jumping at your throat or knocking you down and attacking your head, why, that's no choice at all. Turn your arm so that it's biting down on the outer part rather than the underside, where all the important arteries are. If he bites, don't try to struggle free—that's exactly what angry dogs with powerful snappy jaws want. He'd win with one tug and do terrible damage to your arm in the process.

Instead, push your hand, fist or arm into his mouth to block his airway, make him gag, and confuse him. This is a last resort, as is poking the dog in the eyes with your free hand. If the choice is a severely gnawed hand/arm or a little discomfort to an angry uptight mutt, don't hesitate to push him, poke him, and even punch him if it makes him stop. There really is no code of conduct when it comes to fighting dogs.

And finally, because this incident has already gone on far too long, if he knocks you over and has the choice of what to bite on, remain as calm and motionless as possible. Roll up into a tight ball with your hands over your ears (dogs like eating pigs' ears and yours won't taste dissimilar) and protect your throat with your knees. If he doesn't grow bored by your lifeless body and continues to attack, feed him the arm and prepare to fight dirty.

Survive a shark attack

Statistically, you're more likely to be stung on the ass by a bee than attacked by a shark, but there are always a few bad apples that spoil it for the rest of them by biting, maiming, and eating swimmers. Great Whites, Tiger, Bull, and Oceanic Whitetip sharks all have a history of bothering humans, so do your homework before venturing into their neighborhoods.

According to experts, many shark attacks are merely a case of mistaken identity. They think you're plankton, take a bite, and wander off when you taste wrong, confused and fearful of the threat you present. And, according to those same experts who've dedicated their lives to studying this subject, if you're unfortunate enough to be on the end of a sustained attack, your best bet is to get out of the water. Really. It's as simple as that.

On most occasions, the first the victim is aware of an attack is when the beast comes from nowhere and bites hard on one of their body parts. If you can't clamber out of the water in time, your best bet is to fight back.

Prod and poke their most sensitive areas—the eyes and the gills—like your life depended on it, using any weapon you have on hand. Hit him on the nose if you can't reach the eyes and gills, but be aware that the nose is attached to its mouth, which is full of razor-sharp teeth.

If he attacks then backs off, he may well be waiting for you to die from any injuries he's inflicted. Use the time to plot your route out of the water, but be prepared to defend yourself again. If you're lucky, by denying a shark the upper hand, he's more likely to back down, scamper off, and bother someone else instead.

Sidestep an angry bull

They say that a bull won't bother you unless you bother him, so stay out of his field and you'll be all right. The end.

But what if you have no choice but to trample across his turf? All you can do here is give him as wide a berth as possible, walking calmly and confidently at a brisk, business-like pace.

If he starts to take an interest and you can run to safety, do so as fast as your legs will carry you. That said, never gun it without working out your distances: most bulls running at full speed can move quicker than you and will toss you in the air and trample you underfoot.

If it's all too late and he's making those nasal snorts and scraping his front foot on the ground, your only hope is to make like a matador and whip off your coat or shirt. Bulls are big and powerful with sharp horns, but they're essentially gullible beasts who focus on movement. Hold an item of clothing to one side at arm's length and it will confuse and distract him.

Stand perfectly still and wait. If he charges, toss your makeshift cloak away from you once the bull is within fifteen feet. He'll follow the cloak rather than you, and then become confused by what just happened. This can buy you time to make good your escape.

However, if you're some way from safety, you may have to steal several yards and then repeat the process: take off another item of clothing and confuse him again. Repeat this until you reach the safety of a fence, by which point you could be down to your underpants, which may well be soiled.

An alternative school of thought suggests that a bull can be controlled by grabbing its nose ring and twisting it sharply. Only a moron would try this, and while you may be lacking in certain skills, you're not a moron.

Wrestle an alligator

The easiest way to avoid being clamped between the jaws of a 'gator is to avoid vacationing in Florida and decline any invitation to go out on a small boat across a swamp. We've all seen movies and know how this one ends.

Most alligators are afraid of humans and prefer the safety of water, but they'll still jump out onto land if you show them a leg. If they want to be left alone and you've ventured into their territory, alligators open their mouths and hiss. Don't make him tell you twice—back away rapidly.

The alligators who want to eat you, on the other hand, are likely to emerge from the cover of water at anything up to 30 mph. If he catches you unaware, your best bet is to engage in what's known as a Manly Struggle.

The alligator wants to clamp his jaws down on you, drag you into the water and perform his Death Roll—where he shakes you around until parts of you fall off in bite-sized chunks.

Your only hope is to get on its back as fast as possible, apply downward pressure to its neck so that it can't take a bite, and pray that a game warden with a big gun comes to your rescue.

If the alligator manages to clamp down on a limb, a firm punch to the snout will open up his jaw and allow you to reclaim your body part.

Some experts suggest you cover his eyes as this can make alligators more sedate, while singing a gentle ballad into its ear may also help. But if you only remember one thing from this entry, it should be: keep its jaws shut by applying pressure to its neck and remain on top until help finally arrives. And praying wouldn't hurt, either.

How To...
Tie The Trustiest Knots

Sadly, there is no one-knot-for-all-occasions, just many, many knots that do a number of different jobs. There are at least 350 decent fastenings in existence at the moment, so what follows here are three key knots useful in three important scenarios. Sadly, there wasn't room to include the Corned Beef Knot— used to keep corned beef together during cooking.

A knot to secure stuff

The next time you need to take a cumbersome object from one place to another on top of your car (a suitcase or tree, perhaps), secure it firmly using possibly the easiest fastening ever created: the Reef

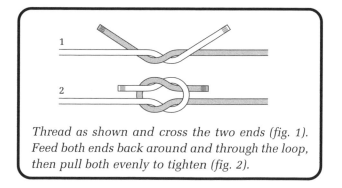

Thread as shown and cross the two ends (fig. 1). Feed both ends back around and through the loop, then pull both evenly to tighten (fig. 2).

Knot. Devised by fishermen, this one's so simple that a twelve-year-old Cub Scout is expected to be able to tie it in his sleep, and should therefore be the default knot of every proper Man.

A knot to tie two ropes together

If you're about to rappel heroically down the side of a building*, look no further than the Double Fisherman's Knot (it being well known that many fishermen like to rappel down buildings in their spare time). It's suitable for tying two lengths of rope together (of either equal or unequal thickness, which is very useful), easy to apply but quite a bit harder to untie afterwards—and that's a good thing as it's less likely to suddenly unravel at 350 feet.

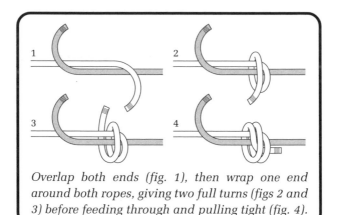

Overlap both ends (fig. 1), then wrap one end around both ropes, giving two full turns (figs 2 and 3) before feeding through and pulling tight (fig. 4).

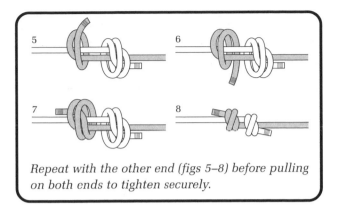

Repeat with the other end (figs 5–8) before pulling on both ends to tighten securely.

We can't recommend rappelling down buildings; it's dangerous. The Double Fisherman's Knot will work just as well for towing a car and lengthening a fishing line, both of which are far safer pursuits.

A knot to tie up a robber up while you wait for the cops

Having hit the intruder over the head with a piece of wood or a cheap vase, two small birds should now be gently twittering above his slumped body. When he comes to in a few minutes he'll either run off into the night or bash your head in and steal your life savings from under your mattress, so you'll need to restrain him until the policemen arrive.

Your best bet is to sit him in a sturdy chair and tie both wrists together with an ultra-secure Constrictor Knot; a loop far easier to apply than it is to undo. Add another Constrictor to each ankle, and warn him that he could do himself some serious damage by attempting to force his hands or legs free. Of course, when the police do finally show up they'll arrest you for assault and let him off with a warning, for the law is indeed a bastard.

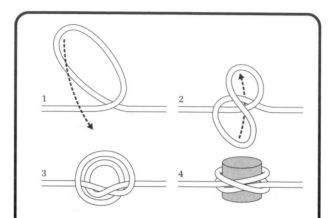

Form a loop with the rope (fig. 1), then continue twisting until the line becomes a figure eight (fig. 2). Twist further until the two ends of the figure eight become individual loops (fig. 3). Place both loops over the hands and tighten (fig. 4). Act fast, in case he regains consciousness.

How To...
Throw Properly
(And Not At All Like A Girl)

It doesn't matter what you're throwing, be it a slobbery tennis ball for a dog or some stones at your neighbor's greenhouse, your manly credentials are on the line with this one.

When throwing anything, anywhere, you'll be judged on two things: distance traveled by the projectile and the ability to complete the toss without looking like a sissy. The following five steps are designed to make sure you score well on both counts...

Step 1. Select your target and stand sideways to it, feet roughly shoulder-width apart to provide a stable base. If you're right-handed, the left foot and arm should both point towards the target, with the arm raised to shoulder height and providing balance. (Obviously you'll need to reverse this if you're left-handed.)

Step 2. Take the throwing arm up at a right angle to just around shoulder height. With the non-throwing arm still focusing on the target, both arms should form an 'L' shape.

Step 3. Now, as the throwing arm swings forward, keep your elbow level with the top of the throwing shoulder. As the weight moves from the back to the front foot, release the ball as the body swings around and the chest faces the target. The perfect trajectory for distance is around 45 degrees; any higher and you'll gain height but lose distance, any lower and the object's arc will be too flat for it to travel far.

Step 4. To avoid a girly finish, when the ball has been released the throwing arm should continue down and across the body so that it finishes next to the hip. If maximum force has been applied, the aiming arm should come down to finish behind the body.

Step 5. If you need extra distance, take a short run up, but make sure you remain balanced and your head stays still and focused on the target right up until the moment it makes contact. A textbook throw. Nothing even slightly sissy about that.

How To...
Navigate By The Stars*

An ancient and fail-safe navigational trick practiced by salty old mariners and alcoholics who wake up underneath bushes. Should you ever find yourself lost in the middle of nowhere, look up to the night sky, wait for your eyes to focus and try to remember which hemisphere you're looking at. This will help you make sense of it all...

If you're lost in the northern hemisphere

Look up and locate two constellations—Ursa Major (aka the the Big Dipper, the Great Bear, and the Saucepan) and Cassiopeia. Ursa Major is a seven-star

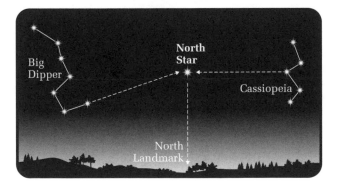

constellation shaped a bit like a farmer's plow, vaguely like a large ladle, nothing at all like a big bear and most of all like a long-handled saucepan. Cassiopeia is less visually imaginative; it's merely five stars that form a 'W' shape hanging vertically.

Both will be visible on a clear night and always sit opposite each other and rotate around the vital North Star (aka Polaris, or Pole Star)—a star that points northward, strangely enough.

To locate the North Star, find the two stars on the right-hand side of the Saucepan. These are 'pointer stars,' so called because if you draw an imaginary line between the two, and then extend that distance roughly five times, the line should reach the North Star. To make certain, before stumbling off due west and into a swamp, check that the North Star is in line with Cassiopeia's center star—the middle peak on the 'W.'

If this all adds up, locate true north by drawing an imaginary line back down vertically from the North Star to earth, and focus the base of the line on some kind of landmark. That way is north, directly behind you is south, and the rest you really ought to be able to work out for yourself.

If you're lost in the southern hemisphere

This is trickier as there are no obvious cooking utensils by which to navigate. Instead, you'll need to find the Southern Cross—four bright stars forming a cross which looks like it's fallen over on its left side. Once located, its pointer stars are the two which would form the long shaft of the cross. To find south, take the distance between the two stars and project it five times as far, moving from left to right. Where the imaginary line ends, draw a line vertically straight down to the horizon and select a landmark to follow. Done correctly, you now have your bearings and can adjust accordingly. Walk on.

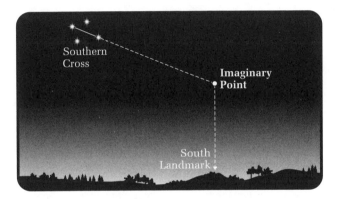

Though the position of the stars in the night sky depends on your location in the world and the time of year you are observing them, the arrangement of these constellations in relation to each other remains constant. You remember that.

How To...
Jump From A
Speeding Train

Sadly, How To...Fight On Top Of A Speeding Train Like They Used To In The Old Days didn't quite make the cut, but the classic 'tumble from a train' was a shoo-in. It used to be that heroic men had no choice but to fling themselves from trains to avoid the carnage of a wreck or escape a man with a gun who wanted them dead. These days you're more likely to use this skill to avoid a ticket taker, but be aware that you can't just go flinging yourself off willy-nilly.

Our lawyers tell us that it's very important to stress that there is no absolutely safe way for average men to jump from a moving train. What there is, though, is the stuntman approach, which minimizes the risk of landing on your head or snapping both legs on impact.

You'll need the train to be travelling at no more than 20 mph, otherwise you'll end up dead. And you'll need to be jumping from a doorway and not a roof, otherwise you'll also end up dead. Apart from that it's a breeze...

The take-off point
A door is normally best for your exit, and preferably an open one. You need enough room to take a small

running jump and a doorway wide enough to get through comfortably. When you push off from your take-off point, make sure your foot is firmly planted to provide you with a good, solid purchase. It will need to push you far enough out of the doorway so that you land safely away from the train rather than on the tracks. Otherwise you'll end up...eh, you get the point.

The target

As you stand at the take-off point, visualize your own little landing zone further down the line. If you've got any sense, make it an area free from rocks, fencing and farmyard animals—delay your jump until soft dirt and a flat surface draws into view. The very best you can hope for is a haystack, or a small, soft, grassy hillock with a slight downward slope away from the tracks. That slope will lessen the impact on contact.

The correct take-off

When you jump, prepare to hit the ground and roll. Land as a parachutist would to cushion the impact: feet together, knees slightly bent, body mildly turned in the air towards the side you want to land on. After that, it's a case of 'assholes and elbows,' according to those in the know. Whatever rolling skills you've picked up over the years will now inevitably take over. Alternatively, if you approach the take-off point and realize that this wasn't one of your brighter ideas, stop, wait for the train to reach the next platform, exit as normal, and pay the fine. Your choice.

How To...
Barbecue Like A Man

Most men are drawn to hot coals like flies to dog crap, yet only a small number know how to barbecue correctly. By correctly, we mean ensuring the meat comes out cooked properly and that none of the guests leaves early because you've poisoned them. Let's start at the beginning...

If you were cooking meat as they did in your great-granddad's day, you'd start your fire by rubbing two sticks together. But because you're an impatient little pyromaniac, you can use a match. The only caveat here is that because no self-respecting man would resort to a gas barbecue, the following rules are written with hand-lit charcoal in mind...

Step 1. Avoid self-lighting or additive-enhanced charcoal, unless you enjoy meat with the unmistakable taste of gas. Additive-free charcoal and natural wood lighters are far better bets and should be built into a nice neat pile in the middle of your barbecue. Bury three paraffin-free lighter cubes in triangle formation among the charcoal, light them, and wait for the flames to spread.

Step 2. If you used lighter fluid to get things moving, you'll need to wait half an hour for their glues and additives to burn off. That's about as long as it takes for the flames to die down and reach a safe temperature to cook your meat anyway, so you can use the time to make any last-minute preparations to your meat, and perhaps to slip on your humorous 'I'd tell you the recipe, but then I'd have to kill you' apron.

Step 3. After thirty minutes the coals should be a dusty white on top of a menacing red glow. This is a good sign. Cooking over raging flames may appear manly, but your meat will end up charred and undercooked, leaving you with a pair of singed eyebrows and a bad case of diarrhea.

Step 4. Never poke and prod at the food with sharp implements as it cooks: it can damage the meat and release the juices, which will leave your meat tasting as dry as an old cardboard box. Instead, use tongs to turn your meat just once during cooking. If you're barbecuing under a lid, you're essentially roasting the meat, so there's no need to turn it at all—it merely slows down the cooking process and irritates hungry people.

Step 5. As a general rule, steak can be cooked as rare as you'd like (see below), but burgers, sausages, and processed meats need to be cooked through until all sign of pink flesh is banished. Chicken is only safe to eat when the juices run clear and there's no sign of pink. Never eat charred meat as its cancer-causing chemicals are bad for you, unless the surgeon general has changed his view on that again.

Know your enemy

Bacteria love a barbecue even more than you do. They flourish in warm temperatures and double their number in twenty minutes, so avoid cross-contamination at all costs, unless you want to vomit until your ears bleed. Beef, particularly burgers, contains a high E. coli threat, while with chicken it's the classic combination of salmonella and campylobacter, so there's potentially something for everyone. Make sure all meat is fully thawed before you begin cooking. Keep the raw and the cooked meat apart to prevent cross-contamination and use two sets of utensils, one for raw, one for cooked. Don't mix these or you might die.

Steak–the rule of thumb (or finger)

Cut the steak open to see if it's cooked and you'll drain it of all its tasty juices. The expert method of testing is to poke the meat as it cooks with your finger, using the following comparisons as your guide.

For rare: hold your hand out, fingers relaxed and naturally apart, then touch the area between thumb and forefinger with your other hand. Press the center of a rare steak and it should feel the same.

For medium: stretch the fingers out further and touch the same flesh again. You've progressed to medium.

For well-done: clench the fist and prod once more. It should now feel tight. You can also feel the front of your nose, you should get the same firmness, unless you have the fat, flabby nose of a raging alcoholic.

How To...
Take A Punch

That psychotic man at the bar has caught you eyeing his girl, and now he wants to administer a sound beating. Blubbing like a child won't cut any ice with this fucker, so you'll have no choice but to defend yourself.

The following might just help you avoid a thorough ass-kicking...*

Your best bet is to try to out-maneuver him and pray someone steps in. Setting yourself up like a boxer gives him less to aim at. Face him with your weaker arm to the front and raised 90 degrees at the elbow to protect your ribs, chest, and face. Your punching arm should be furthest away from him, while your feet need to be firmly planted to give you a strong, solid base—but be ready to move quickly as he moves towards you.

As the fight unfolds:

If he throws a straight jab...
Block his punch with your arm on the same side as it's being thrown. If it gets through, aim to meet it with your forehead. This may sound preposterous, but if he's going to land a punch on your pretty face you're far better off attempting to absorb the blow with the hardest part of your head, rather than your soft nose or vulnerable chin. Also, if he lands one with your head moving backwards, you'll feel the full force and stand more chance of being knocked off your feet. Tighten your neck muscles and jaw, and clench your teeth at the moment of impact. If your mouth is open and he lands a punch, the chances of it knocking you out and breaking your jaw increase.

Hit back with...
A hook. You can't dance around him all night, and hitting back is self-defense in this instance. So, protect your head with your left hand (provided you're right-handed) and by dropping your chin down to the middle of your left shoulder. As your right arm comes around his hands, turn your hand over so the palm is facing down and four knuckles land flush on the side of his head. Don't feel bad, you told him you didn't actually 'want some.'

If he throws an uppercut...

If he lands cleanly this could do serious damage to your chin or nose and dangerously whip your head back in the process, so try to block it with your arm and step to one side.

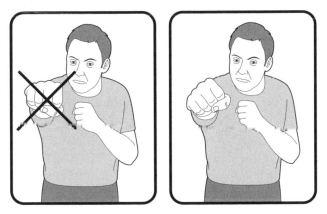

Turn the fist slightly as you make contact. If you land your punch straight, you're likely to damage your hand.

Hit back with...

A straight jab to the face. Even though it's a straight punch, the fist should never land flat against his face or you risk doing your hand and wrist as much damage. Turn it so that it lands on his chin at a 45-degree angle.

If he throws a hook...

If this lands on the side of your head, it could do damage to your jaw and ear. Unless he's highly trained (in which case ignore these instructions and run away), he'll likely telegraph this particular shot, lurching back and giving you time to take the force of the blow on the forearm or elbow—imagine combing your hair as the punch is thrown because the action of blocking it with your arm is the same. You could also move in closer and allow his punch to fall behind your head, and, in theory, 'roll' underneath his punch. The latter takes clever timing and could result in you taking a knee to the face, which will suck.

Hit back with…
An uppercut. Lower your right shoulder to drop the right side of your body, keeping your left hand up to protect your chin. Rotate your hips forward and step into the punch, bringing your shoulder forwards and up. The arm should stay close to the body through-out and the punch should land underneath his jaw, with the palm of your hand facing your chest as you finish. That'll teach him.

If he goes for the body…
He could well kill you by landing a punch down below. If you see it coming, bring your elbows down while turning away from the shot. If you have no other option, move to the side slightly to take the shot on your obliques—the muscles on your sides which cover the ribs. This will still hurt, but at least you'll avoid damage to your vital organs. Never suck your stomach in if you see the shot coming, as you'll leave those vital organs exposed.

Hit back with...
A hook (see above). It should be over by now, one way or another. If not, keep doing what you've been doing. He'll run out of steam soon. Probably.

This skill assumes the assailant is up for a fair fight, one based very loosely on rules of professional boxing. If you suspect he's carrying a pool ball in a sock, scream like a child and run.**
**Unless you happen to be really hard, in which case you don't need instructions.

Disclaimer: this entry covers the very basics of self-defense and is clearly no substitute for being taught boxing properly, by experts. The publishers cannot condone fighting; it solves nothing and you may well end up on the wrong end of a righteous beating. You have been warned.

How To...
Deal With A Nasty Cut

What started out as high jinks has escalated into horseplay and ended with an accident and blood everywhere. It's all very regrettable, but before the finger of blame can be pointed, it needs to stop gushing blood. Assess the situation. If the finger (or arm or whatever it is) is now hanging off by a thread, this is a job for a trained doctor, not you. If there's no threat of death by bleeding you can deal with it yourself by following these simple enough steps...

Step 1. Take a clean cloth and press it gently onto the wound. This is mainly to stop the blood from spurting out, but also to encourage the clotting process to begin.

Step 2. The heart pumps blood through the body, as you may already know. To reduce the supply to the wound, hold it above the level of the heart as soon as possible. For that reason, the victim should lie down on the floor, with their head lowered, feet raised, and any tight clothing loosened, so much as taste and decency allows.

Step 3. Apply a dressing to the wound—which, in a

pinch, need not be anything more medicinal than a clean towel held in place by a bandage. Resist the urge to keep checking under the dressing to see if the blood has stopped bubbling; if anything, this will cause it to bleed more. And if the blood soaks through, simply apply another pad on top.

Step 4. Reassure the victim that it's not as bad as it feels, unless it is, in which case you should be almost at the hospital by now instead of reading this far down the page. If the bleeding still shows no sign of slowing, call an ambulance immediately. If the clotting has begun, run the wound under a tap, dry, and apply a light bandage. Nature will take care of the rest.

How to treat a really nasty burn

In this regrettable incident, someone has been left with a nasty burn. If it's any larger than a silver dollar, proceed directly to the hospital. Provided it's not ridiculously deep, anything smaller can usually be treated simply and effectively by the average man.

Place the burn under cold water for ten minutes to reduce pain and distress–this may also leave less of a mark on the skin.

To reduce the risk of infection, wrap the burn in gauze and allow the area to continue cooling. Left open to the air, the wound will be more uncomfortable and infection could end up with the limb falling off; although–yes–that is definitely a worst-case scenario, with no real evidence to support it.

How To...
Gut A Fish

You've caught your dinner using the Catch A Fish With A Piece Of String skill on page 73, now you'll need to remove its innards before you fry it in a pan—otherwise it won't taste at all pleasant. These instructions presume that you're simply looking for a nice meal, preferably one without the head staring back at you. (If you do want a fancy presentation fish, served up on a silver platter, see the box for instructions.) So, with a blunt instrument at the ready, follow these steps in this order...

Step 1. If the fish is still squirming, hold it tight with one hand and crack it over the head, just behind the eyes, with a blunt instrument. It's kinder than gutting him alive and the knife is easier to wield if he's not wriggling around and trying to escape. Clean off any blood before you begin the gutting process.

Step 2. Use a sharp knife to shear the pectoral fins off on either side.

Step 3. Using short strokes, run the knife's dull edge along the fish's flanks at a flat, 90-degree angle. If it runs smoothly the scales won't pose a problem and can stay. If there's resistance and the scales pop up,

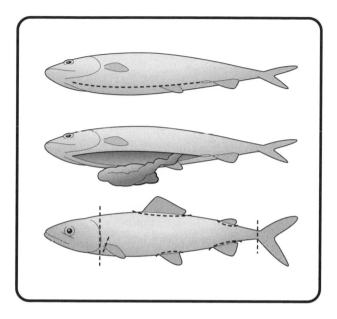

as they will with most salmon and trout, scrape them off until the fish is smooth.

Step 4. The fun stuff starts here, providing your idea of fun is running a knife up through a dead fish's anus. Insert the point of the knife into the 'vent' (anus), and slice along the underside of the fish, past its belly, all the way up under the jaw and the gills (the flaps it once used for breathing, before you bludgeoned its brains out).

Step 5. Open the fish and remove its guts—use the knife to cut through the sinewy parts and remove the no-longer-vital organs. Then take the tip of a knife and dig out the dark reddish-brown kidney line running along the backbone, which will make the fish taste muddy if you leave it in. Rinse the fish out thoroughly, just to be sure.

Step 6. Cut off its head just below the gills, then trim off the tail where it joins the body. Finish by cutting off any other fins the fish may have (this varies between the species) as well as the dorsal fin (the big one on the top)—it's full of little bones and doesn't taste nice. Cut either side of the fin and tug from the tail end outward to pull the fin and its bones out. What remains should be cooked and eaten with French fries (serving suggestion).

How to present swanky fish

To impress guests at a fancy dinner party, you may prefer to present the fish as a whole (minus its guts, obviously) on a big silver platter. To do this, ignore steps 1, 2, and 6—don't remove the scales, fins, gills or head, and when you slice into the fish's underside, cut up to and behind the gills on either side until the head is held on only by the backbone. Serve to gasps of amazement, perhaps ditching greasy French fries and having some nice potatoes and some fresh vegetables instead.

How To...
Throw A Boomerang

At first glance this could have been held back for the follow-up publication to this book: *Pointless Skills*. However, delve a little deeper and you'll discover that a boomerang can be used as a weapon for hunting and fighting, an impromptu percussion instrument and, apparently, as a fire starter. So for any man who ever needs to fight a pig to the death, play a celebratory tune on its ribs, and then cook it to a lovely crisp over a raging fire, the boomerang is essential.

Should you also wish to throw the boomerang away and watch it return for no other reason than it might be mildly entertaining, well, this magic stick can do that too...

Step 1. Find yourself an open space, but before you set up, make sure there are no toddlers, ice sculptures, or workmen carrying a large pane of glass back and forth across your path. If the coast is clear, grip the boomerang with the flat side to the palm, with the (near) end sitting around the middle of the palm, being supported by the thumb and first two fingers. The tip of the boomerang should then rest on the top of your third finger.

Step 2. Raise the wood above your shoulder and throw it straight forward in an upright position (see fig. 1). If you're right-handed, angle the boomerang approximately 10 degrees to the right (10 degrees to the left for the left-handed minority). The angle at which you throw the boomerang depends on strength of the wind (fig. 2). If it's blowing hard, angle the boomerang a little more inward; if it's calm, angle it a little further outward. Trial and error will tell you how far to go—but never throw it vertically upright.

Step 3. Resist the temptation to throw the boomerang up in the air—it will climb by itself, as if by magic—so aim no more than 20 degrees above the horizon. Finally, never throw from a standing position, with your feet just sitting there side by side. If you're right-handed, make sure your left foot is stepping forward as you throw (and vice versa for lefties), then apply a flick of your wrist to give it as much spin as possible as it leaves your hand. Thanks to advanced physics too tedious and complex to go into here, when you let go the boomerang should 'right'

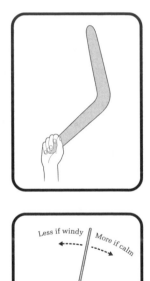

Less if windy   More if calm

0° – 30°

itself as it commences its turn and return to you spinning in the horizontal position. But what if...oh crap...it's arcing straight back for your head!

Step 4. Fear not. Simply follow its path and prepare yourself to catch it at the side of your body by clasping it in the palms of both hands (fig. 3) as it passes by. Unless you enjoy the taste of blood and broken teeth, never attempt to catch the boomerang at face level, and only attempt to catch it one-handed if you're a raging jackass.

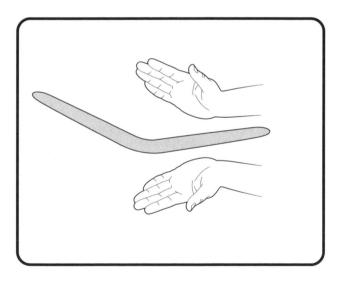

A few words of warning

1. Throwing a boomerang straight into a strong wind is asking for trouble, especially if it blows straight back towards your delicate face. Anything over 5 mph is considered 'too strong'. If in doubt, lick your finger, raise it to the wind and pull a face that suggests you're assessing the conditions. After a second or two, shake your head and suggest opening the picnic basket instead.

2. Always wait until the sky is clear before throwing. Kites, low-flying aircraft, hovering birds of prey, and other boomerangs clogging up the airways will all conspire to screw up your attempt.

3. Keep your eye on the boomerang throughout the throw. If it arcs back towards you, prepare to catch safely (see main copy, and also the warning below). If it flies off and shows no sign of returning, follow its path to where it finally rests or risk losing your precious magic stick forever.

4. If the boomerang is arcing back towards you, but appears to have picked up too much speed as it hones in on your head, turn your back on it, bend over, and protect your skull with your arms. Otherwise it may take your head clean off.

Warning: This advice is only valid for boomerangs designed to be thrown rather than used as overpriced decorative trinkets bought by gullible Down Under tourists, which aren't designed to be thrown.

How To...
Pull A Tooth

The swinging door method was very popular in the days of black-and-white films, when brave men were driven to the edge of insanity by a throbbing tooth. You could always pull a rotten tooth out using pliers, of course, but that's far less impressive than employing the swinging door method. All you'll need is a line of string, a door and a high pain threshold...

Open wide!

The line needs to be fine enough to tie first around your chosen tooth, then around the door knob, but robust enough not to snap when the door is slammed shut.

Said door should be heavy enough to provide the force needed to yank the tooth clean out.

Work out how far away you'll need to stand so that when the door shuts the line becomes taut, then anaesthetize the pain you're about to feel with strong booze. Plant both feet firmly on the ground and swing the door hard towards its fra...eh? What's this?

Ah, it says here that under no circumstances whatsoever should any man (or woman) ever attempt to pull his own tooth, and particularly not using the irresponsible Line-Of-String-And-Swinging-Door Technique.

Apparently, even if the tooth is loose, the bone holding it in place will still be strong. By pulling it out, either using the door or a pair of pliers, you'll almost certainly break off the top of the tooth, spread the infection, possibly break your jaw, and maybe end up with a life-threatening abscess, having first gone into shock due to the trauma of it all. If you're unable to stop the blood loss, you're likely to need transfusions, unless you die first.

Alternatively...
So, an alternative approach, of course, is to contact a dentist in your neighborhood and make an emergency appointment. They'll either operate, prescribe drugs to numb the pain, or otherwise fix the problem in a way that leaves you with full use of your mouth.

How To...
Pull Off A Card Trick

Every man should know just one card trick that will keep innocent children and gullible women entertained. However, mastering any more than one 'sleight of hand' marks you as an eccentric loner with too much time on his hands. (Learning 'just one more' is probably how it started for that oddball David Blaine.)

So, if you're only going to learn one trick, make it one of the easiest in the book: the Card In The Wallet trick. You'll allow your victim to pick a card from the pack, any card at all. Then, through a combination of cunning trickery and outright deceit, you'll pull the very same card they plucked from the deck out of your wallet.

The preparation

In case you hadn't guessed, you'll need two decks of cards, which will give you two of the same card. Any card will suffice, but for the purpose of this example we'll use the Jack of Diamonds.

Put one of these Jacks in your wallet. Now, add a small square of double-sided tape on the underside of the wallet and put it away in your pocket. Put the other Jack on the top of the deck and prepare to make magic happen.

The trick

Pull the wallet out, making certain the tape is hidden from view, and announce that inside lies a miracle—or some other such magic hocus-pocus crap. Be warned, though, that if anyone sees the tape, your trick is well and truly screwed and you'll look like the charlatan you are.

But they haven't seen the tape, so fan the cards out towards them and ask them to remove any card from anywhere in the deck*—but not to look at it. Take the card from them and put it face down on top of the deck.

Now bring in more smoke and mirrors. In order to distract your prey, stare into their eyes and ramble on once more about miracles happening, and how you will soon reveal to them the card they chose: at the same time, and without being observed (and that bit's very important), place the wallet (tape-side down) on top of the deck. Press down firmly on it so that now, as you pick the wallet back up, the tape picks up the victim's card and leaves the Jack of Diamonds on top of the deck.

Now, announce that your victim must turn over the card they'd picked. As they do so, and the Jack is revealed, they'll believe this to be the card they chose.

Finally, open your wallet and whip out the stashed second Jack (keeping the underside of the wallet—and the card stuck there—well concealed). Now, unless something's gone badly wrong, you should have hood-winked the fool (or child). Announce 'that's magic!' in a squeaky voice, keeping to yourself that it's really nothing more than low-level deceit.

If the victim selects the card on top of the pile, panic not. Simply proceed as normal, but skip the sticky tape procedure at the end.

How To...
Whistle Through Your Fingers

The shrill toot of the magical finger whistle is not only an essential skill for any dog fans reading, it's also good for when...erm, if you need to...er... Actually, summoning dogs is about all it is good for, but one toot and that mutt will know who's in charge.

The technique

Step 1. Form a 'U' or 'V' shape with your fingers by loosely touching the ends of your bent index finger and thumb.

Step 2. Rest your fingers (if you're using your right hand, the thumb should be to the right) on your lower teeth.

Step 3. The tips of your fingers should be resting against the bottom front part of your tongue, and pushing it back into your mouth so it rests just behind your bottom row of teeth.

Step 4. Press your lips down against your fingers, which form the 'U' or 'V' into which you must blow.

The sound is created by your upper teeth and tongue forcing air onto the lower lip and teeth. Apparently.

Step 5. As you blow, you may initially find that you're making nothing more than a pitiful wheezing noise which leaves your fingers covered in spittle. Keep practicing and fine-tuning the position of your fingers, and you should soon possess a shrill whistle, plus a dozen dogs by your side.

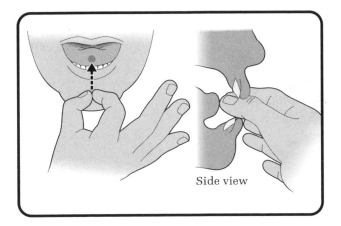

Side view

How To...
Survive A Car
Emergency

You're just driving down the road, minding your own business, well within the speed limit and dutifully respecting all the other vehicles on the road, when…ah crap…we appear to have a problem…

Your tire blows

It's very easy to say this from here, but try not to panic. If the tire blows, particularly a front tire, your car will try to take you in a different direction from the one you're trying to go in (presumably, forward)—toward the damaged wheel.

The worst thing you could ever do is slam on the brakes in a blind panic. You'll end up with a tattooed truck driver plowing straight up your ass, or worse. If there is worse. And there probably isn't.

Instead of panicking, gently ease off the gas, keeping your hands firmly clamped on the wheel in the '10 and 2' position. As you ease off, try to remember where the hazard light switch is and flick it on, then go down through the gears to slow the car as you move it safely to the side of the road.

Once you've slowed to a safe speed, apply the brake gently, bring the car to a halt and breathe deeply.

The engine fails!

Why and how the engine has failed is not really the most pressing issue at this moment in time, as it's all very technical. Yes, you're right, I don't have the first clue, but all you really need to know is how to react anyway, damnit. Luckily, this one's fairly simple: put the car into neutral, signal your intentions, and brake gently. Without the engine's assistance, braking and steering takes more effort, but compared to a blowout this is a cakewalk. Reduce speed until you can pull off the road safely. Stop. Switch ignition off. Switch on hazard warning lights and get out. Call AAA. Wait a millennia. Call again and ask what's taking so long. Wait some more. Prepare to pay out the ass.

You're starting to skid!!

The road is snowy, icy, or just wet, and without warning your car starts to skid. The most unexpected skids occur on wet roads, with what's known as hydroplaning. When this happens, a layer of water between the tires and the road surface reduces the tires' friction and, therefore, their grip. That's the technical stuff; here's how to save your ass.

Resist the natural urge to hit the brakes—you'll be face first in a ditch before you can mutter 'Oh crap.' Instead, depress the clutch, ease off the accelerator, and simply (and smoothly) steer into the direction of the skid until you've regained control of the car.

In wintery conditions, preparation is often the key. If there's snow on the ground or there's a decent chance of ice being on the roads, you should be wearing comfortable footwear at the wheel rather than snow boots, to give you greater control on the pedals. You should also be driving at a much slower, safe speed, avoiding any sudden jerky movements and reducing your rate of travel to a retiree's Sunday drive as you approach any bends.

You'll have checked the pressure and tread depth of your tires before venturing out (3 mm tread is OK, less than 2 mm is asking for trouble), and obviously you'll have packed a shovel in the trunk in case you get snowed under, and a nice flask of soup. Diligent preparation is admittedly a hassle, but at least you'll reach your destination in one piece and with the warm glow of satisfaction that only a good cream of mushroom can give.

The effing accelerator's jammed!!!

If this happens, you can consider yourself very unlucky indeed. But there's no time to cry about it, as you'll need to have your wits about you if you're to avoid a major accident. Fortunately, if you can stop carrying on like a girl, it's not too difficult to come to a safe stop.

Shift the gears into neutral, apply the brakes gently, put on your turn signal and steer to the side of the road. Only then, when the car's stationary, should you turn the ignition off. Try turning it off in a blind panic while you're driving (in the not unreasonable hope that it will cut the engine) and you may lock the steering, making an already tricky job a whole lot harder. Once the car has stopped safely, turn the ignition off as soon as humanly possible, otherwise you'll inflict serious damage on your engine (which is probably at this point revving itself hoarse, given the car's still in neutral). Switch on those hazard lights and call AAA. By now you should have their number on speed-dial.

And the brakes have failed!!!!

Oh fuck, this one's not good. Think fast, act sharp, and keep your eyes on the road at all times. Firstly, try pumping the brake pedal, and if you're very lucky, the pressure may come back long enough to enable you to stop safely.

If it doesn't, slowly apply the emergency brake and drop down into a lower gear, and the added drag should slow the car down and allow you to pull over at a safe stopping point. Never try this on a corner, however, as the car could spin out of control. The key with this skill is to act as quickly, but calmly, as possible. Survive this and you've escaped every car-based emergency imaginable. Surely.

Oh shit, to top it all off, now the hood has flown open!!!!!

You'd have to laugh, were it not for the fact you can't see that you're about to wrap your car around a tree. The worst reaction, as usual, is to slam on the brakes—the vehicles behind will plow straight into you. A better bet is to begin slowing gently and look-ing to see if the road ahead is visible in the gap between the dashboard and the hood. If not, you'll need to do the Dog Maneuver and stick your head out of the window to see what's ahead of you, with your slobbery tongue sticking out an optional extra. Slow down smoothly, pull off to the side of the road and think hard about buying a more reliable car.

How To...
Eat Lobster

You've bought, caught, or ordered a nice big lobster for dinner, and he's currently being boiled alive on the stove. The only problem is that you're somewhat inexperienced when it comes to fine dining and you've never eaten the king of crustaceans before. You wouldn't know a telson from a tomalley, nor which part to snap and what you should suck. Luckily, here's a short cut. Allow him to cool after cooking, poke him with your fork to make sure he's dead, then attack in the following order...

Step 1. Hold the back and twist off the legs. They contain minuscule morsels which can be scraped or sucked straight out like a fishy straw.

Step 2. Break off the claws by twisting them at the joints. Bend the thumby claw back to separate it from the crusher and scrape out the meat inside the shell. Use a nutcracker or heavy knife to break the crusher claw and plunder the meat inside.

Step 3. Twist the tail into two parts, then break off the tail flippers (which contain the aforementioned telson) and extract what little meat they contain. The main piece of tail contains the lobster's tastiest meat. Push the tail meat out and on to your plate in one piece, peeling off and discarding the dirty black vein that runs the length of this section.

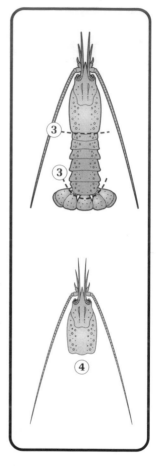

Step 4. Tackling the main body is generally only for the fearless. Grip it at the hole left where you removed the tail and pull the shell away from the body. Inside you'll find the gills, the circulation system and the green digestive gland (that tomalley thing). If it's a female lobster, there may also be unfertilized eggs. The tomalley and the eggs are both edible, if you're not fussy and still hungry.

Step 5. Even if you'll eat anything and are still peckish after steps 1 to 4, avoid the antenna, antennules and the big beak at all costs. They're inedible and would give you indigestion and terrible gas.

How To...
Mend A Bike Tire

That hissing sound isn't the pleasing noise of a bottle of beer being opened; it's a giant dirty nail stuck in your bicycle tire. It will soon be joined by the sound of steam billowing angrily from your ears when you realize that you now have no choice but to carry the thing home in a childlike huff and set about fixing the puncture...

You'll need:
- 1 puncture-repair kit or spare inner tube
- 2 tire levers, available from all good bike shops
- 1 spanner to release the wheel (unless it's a quick-release model)
- 1 air pump

Ready to operate
Step 1. Flip the bike on its head and remove the nut or the quick-release lever to take off the wheel. Use the tire levers to pry the tire from the rim section by section, until the tire and inner tube come free.

Step 2. Run your hands around the inside of the tire to check for the nail or whatever it was was that spoiled your fun. Remove the offending object and study it closely for a few moments, mutter an expressive expletive, then cast it aside while you check the rest of the tire to make sure there are no other pointy things left in there.

Step 3. Find the hole in the inner tube either by pumping it up or holding it under water—the bubbles will give it away. Mark it with a pen or chalk with a cross over the hole. Taking the emery paper from your puncture-repair kit and scuff the area around the hole until the middle of the cross is erased completely—this will make it easier to secure the glue to the inner tube. And now, even though the center of the cross has been scuffed away, the four ends should still point you to the center (and therefore the hole).

Step 4. Spread a penny-sized blob of glue evenly around the hole, making sure it's bigger than the puncture-repair-kit patch. Let it dry until it feels tacky, then apply a small blob of glue to the underside of the patch, place the patch over the hole and push it down firmly for at least a minute. Wait for a couple of minutes more before carefully peeling off the backing.

Step 5. Check the inside edge of the outer tire again to make sure there are no sharp pointy things lurking there, then pump just enough air into the inner tube to give it a nice wheel-shaped shape; don't forget to push the valve stem through the rim's hole. While snickering childishly at that previous phrase, make sure the valve fits through comfortably to avoid any later complications. Now push the tube into the rim all the way around, making sure it's not twisted.

Step 6. Work the outer tire back over the wheel rim, using the tire levers or your fingers to make sure it's in all the way around. Pump more air in to make sure that the tube isn't caught between the rim and the tire. Reattach the wheel and pump it up fully.

Step 7. Realize that you could have avoided steps 1 to 6 altogether by paying a man in the bike shop $20 to do it for you. Then accept that it wouldn't have made much of an entry. What's that you say? Eh? Oh. Yes, fair point.

How To...
Cook The Fish You Caught On Page 73
[And Gutted On Page 168]

Unless you're a Japanese guy, you'll want to cook your fish before you eat him. (If you are a Japanese lad, please ignore this entry and turn the page—raw fish holds no fear for you.)

We're assuming you're still stuck out in the wilderness, living on your wits and by now sporting a large straggly beard that's starting to smell slightly off. Unfortunately, because you forgot to bring salt, pepper, garlic butter, and your handcrafted revolving spice rack, it's plain fish for dinner again, cooked over a crackling fire with only the flies for company.

Fish spoils soon after death, particularly when it's hot and humid outside. Eat a rotten fish and as revenge for killing him and whipping out his guts expect vomiting, paralysis, and a terrible case of diarrhea. So clearly you'll need to act fast.

Having gutted him you could, in theory, cook your fish over the hot coals of a simple fire, but for that you'd need to cook it in thick aluminum foil, which you may not have, or banana leaves, if you're slumming it in a Latin American forest. Simply wait for the flames to die down and for the coals to turn white and smoldering before shoving the fish on to cook. Give him ten minutes per 2.5 cm of thickness, and turn halfway through. Unwrap and eat, probably with your fingers.

Alternatively...

For the man with no foil or thick leaves on-hand, your best bet is to impale Mr. Fish on a clean stick, make several large slashes across his skin to ensure the flesh cooks more evenly throughout, and hold him over the hot coals for a few minutes, taking care not to burn him to a tasteless crisp. To check that he's cooked, cut into the back of the fish and the flesh next to the bone should be opaque, not translucent. When he's done, eat him.

How To...
Mix A Killer Cocktail

For those occasions when a forty ounce of Olde English and a wine cooler don't seem appropriate...

For Her...a Cosmopolitan

The one that those women drink in that TV show.

Ingredients
Citrus vodka
Cointreau (or triple sec)
Fresh lime juice
Cranberry juice
Ice cubes
25ml measuring cup
Cocktail shaker
Cocktail glass
Strainer
One fresh orange
Cigarette lighter

Instructions

1. Pour 1 measure citrus vodka, 1/2 measure of Cointreau, 1 measure fresh lime juice, and 1 measure cranberry juice into cocktail shaker. Fill with ice and shake, having put the top on the shaker first.

2. Strain contents into a cocktail glass.

3. Cut a small slice of orange peel, and warm the skin side with the cigarette lighter. Hold the peel over the center of the drink and squeeze over the flame—oil from the peel should ignite and create a bright yellow flame. Wipe the rim of the glass with the orange peel and drop it into the glass. Serve.

For Him...a dry Martini
The king of all cocktails.

Ingredients
Dry vermouth
Gin or vodka (your choice, sir)
Ice cubes
Cocktail glass
Mixing glass
25ml measuring cup
Long-handled bar spoon
Strainer
Cocktail olives
Cocktail sticks (optional)
One fresh lemon

Instructions

1. Put the ice cubes into a cocktail glass and cover them with cold water. This will chill the glass nicely.

2. Fill the mixing glass with ice and pour in a little dry vermouth. Stir for several seconds with the bar spoon and then strain off the vermouth and excess water. This way the ice gets coated with vermouth and the mixing glass gets chilled.

3. Add 3 measures of gin or vodka into the mixing glass over the remaining ice and stir well.

4. Empty the chilled water from the cocktail glass and strain in the gin or vodka.

5. Garnish with 3 cocktail olives on a stick or use a knife to cut a little piece of lemon peel and squeeze the oil from the peel on top of the drink.

6. Make a lemon twist by cutting a strip of peel into a quarter-inch-thick strip and twist like a corkscrew. Wipe the rim of the glass with it and drop it into the Martini. Now guzzle the glass dry.

How To...
Fix A Leaky Faucet

A leaky faucet can test the patience of any man. Water experts claim that even a slight drip can drain almost 40 gallons of water a week, which is a good 28 buckets. Extrapolate that over three years and you'd have enough water to fill your own private lake and adjoining water park.

Obviously a leaking faucet costs you money, but it can also stain your sink or bath and deprive you of sleep in the darkest hours with that incessant drip, drip, effing drip. Oh Christ, when will it ever stop?! It'll effing stop when you bother to replace the washer (available for a few dollars from all DIY stores), because that's all it normally takes...

Before you begin, however, avoid being sprayed in slapstick comedy fashion by turning the water supply off. The stop valve responsible for this is normally located close to where the water pipe enters the building. It's often, but not always, under the sink—locate it in advance before you need it in an emergency.

Turn on the sink tap to remove any water lurking in the pipes. When it runs dry turn it off and put the drain cover in to prevent those small parts you will

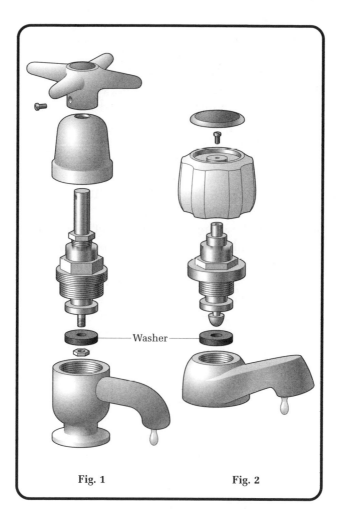

Fig. 1   Fig. 2

inevitably drop from falling down the drain.

For the regular, conventional tap (fig. 1), you'll need to carefully remove the top by unscrewing the little nut by hand or with a wrench. If it's a more modern tap (fig. 2), the screw will be concealed under the hot and cold tap heads.

If you unscrew the nut using a wrench, shove a cloth underneath to avoid scratching your nice shiny tap, and when undoing the hexagonal nut, hold the tap to prevent it from rotating and screwing up your sink or bathtub.

Taps vary and the washer will either be in the headgear you've just removed or on the valve seating (the shelf on which the washer sits) still attached to the tap. It may also be held in place by a small retaining nut, which will need unscrewing. The old washer will look like the new washer, only older and much less shiny.

Pry it off and attach the new one, then reverse the instructions above to screw the headgear back on to the tap, taking care not to over-tighten.

Turn the water supply back on and if the dripping has stopped, this entry is finished for you. Congratulations.

If it's still as bad as it was before, the valve seating may be worn or coated with limescale. Invest in a valve-seat grinder (also available from DIY stores), push the end into the tap and twist to clean the metal work and provide a flat, flush surface for the washer to sit on.

Reassemble as above, and if the drip still continues, lose your temper totally, then call a plumber who can end this sorry charade once and for all. Ah well, at least you tried.

How To...
Change A Tire

That funny rumbling noise and the overall lopsided feel to your car suggests one of your tires is flat. This can't be ignored by turning up the radio, so you'll have to put on your spare. Here's what to do...

Spare change

To minimize the damage to the wheel, slow down to a grandma's pace (5 mph should do) and pull off to a safe place. (To minimize possible damage to yourself, make sure you haven't pulled over near any gun-wielding maniacs.)

Turn off the engine, make sure the hazard lights are on and apply the emergency brake—if it's a manual car, put it in reverse. If it's an automatic, put it in park.

Remove luggage and passengers to lighten the load, and put down one of those warning-triangle things, if you're one of the few people who actually owns one. This will discourage truck drivers from plowing into you, provided they haven't dropped off after thirty-seven straight hours at the wheel. If they have, the triangle won't save you.

Now check to find your spare tire (it's normally in the trunk, underneath the floorboards) and the essential tools you will need—a lug wrench and jack, plus your car's owner's manual. Without these you can't proceed and will need to call for help or extend your thumb toward the slow lane. If you have all the parts, you're ready to begin...

The beginning

Step 1. First, you need to remove the hubcap, which is the metal disk that covers the center of the wheel —unless you have alloy wheels, in which case this instruction doesn't apply and you've just wasted seven seconds you'll never get back. Pry it off with your fingers or with the end of the lug wrench. If you're using the wrench, give the wheel nuts a half-turn counterclockwise. To keep the wheel stable and balanced, unscrew them diagonally (unscrew one, then the one diagonally opposite to it—try to keep up). If the nuts are particularly stiff, either coat them with a little oil and leave for a few minutes, or hold one end of the wrench with your hand and step on the other end with your giant foot.

Step 2. Your manual should suggest the safest, sturdiest lifting point on the car to place the jack. If the jack point is anything less than perfectly secure then you, stupid fool, are asking for trouble—jacks can easily slip, even on flat surfaces.

When the jack is in place, insert the handle and slowly turn it to raise the car. You'll need to jack it just high enough for the damaged wheel to still be touching the ground, but far enough for the spare tire to slide flat under the car's body. If the car does slip off the jack, the tire will at least cushion the blow. Keep jacking up until the flat tire is just clear of the road, then continue to unscrew the nuts in diagonal pairs and remove them. Place them in your pocket and keep them safe. In your pocket.

Step 3. Remove the wheel, which will be heavy and coated in a combination of oil, dirt, and probably some dead vermin. Place it under the raised edge of the car for cushioning (having obviously moved the spare tire first). Stick the good tire onto the hub, the right way around, and fit the nuts on in diagonal formation again, tightening with your fingers for now. The nuts, yes. Didn't you put them in your pocket …?

Use the jack to lower the car until the tire just touches the ground, then tighten the nuts properly and refit the wheel trim.

The end

Shove the damaged tire in the trunk, lower the car fully and remove the jack. Refill the car with bags and people, signal to rejoin traffic, and maneuver on your way.

Ditch the doughnuts

If your spare is what those in the trade call a 'spacesaver' or 'doughnut,' it's a temporary tire designed only to get you to the nearest garage, where an oily mechanic will replace it with a sturdier model. Never exceed 40 mph on a temporary tire–and replace the damaged tire asap.

And with your safety in mind, never, ever attempt to change a wheel on the hard shoulder of a highway–a semi could very easily take your head off. Put your hazard lights on, call AAA and stand a safe distance (30 feet or so) behind the car and away from the road.

How To...
Buy Her A Present She Might Actually Like For Once

How would I know? I've never even met her. However, if she's anything like most women then you'd do well to listen to her a bit more, and try to retain at least some of the information she tells you. Pay particular attention in the weeks before birthdays and Christmas when she's guaranteed to drop hints.

However, if you've had your fingers in your ears for the last few months and have been totally oblivious to all her pointers, you'll need to do some homework. The first sensible thing to do is to ask her best friend, who will normally know exactly what to suggest and will be flattered to be consulted (and will of course tell your lady friend all about how sweetly bumbling you were afterwards. For some reason, they like that kind of thing.) Don't ask her mom, however, unless you actively want your future mother-in-law to think you are an unimaginative, unromantic, lazy ass. It's also worth making a surreptitious pass through the latest issue of your lady's favorite magazine, which will usually give you a few clues as to what's 'in' and 'out' this month, not to mention a better understanding of acceptable penis dimensions.

Still stuck for ideas? Sadly, there are no one-size-fits-all rules where women are concerned; they're a complicated breed. However, exhaustive studies have revealed that the following gifts rev most lady engines:

- Anything you've put a bit of thought and effort into—which rules out almost everything you can buy from the gas station the night before her big day. Think girly: an album of special photos, perhaps, even if most of the pics show her and her friends more than a little plastered in a karaoke bar. An old-fashioned mix tape of her favorite songs, or some hard-to-find, cherished book from her childhood will also score highly.
- A home-made 'voucher' of some kind— whether it's for a no-expenses-spared dinner for two followed by a night in a trendy hotel or a simple 'I promise to babysit, shop, clean, cook, wash up and wait on you for a whole weekend so you can put your feet up.' Consider it a role reversal, for she certainly will.
- Any luxury item she would never normally justify splurging on—a cashmere sweater (or scarf, if you're a cheapskate), a hand-stitched,

leather-bound notebook, or even a selection of really good-quality chocolates from a proper chocolatier (go for an over-priced Belgian box, rather than Esther Price).

- An unusual, unexpected day out—a day at the races, a picnic by the sea, a trip up the river in a nice boat, a night at the opera, an afternoon at a swanky spa, that kind of thing.

- Perfume, jewelry, flowers and lingerie are always popular, but can be a bitch to get right. With your lady's undergarments, make sure you got the right size, even if it means snooping through her underwear drawer on the sly. Never allow her to catch you snooping through her underwear drawer, of course, and remember you're buying said panties for her, not you. If it looks like a frilly wire hanger, its probably not been designed with her comfort in mind.

And buying her a present when it's not an 'occasion' wouldn't hurt either—the element of surprise and all that.

How To...
Clean The Windows
Like A Pro

If you can no longer see the mailman approaching due to a build-up of grime and bird crap, it's probably about time to give the windows a quick once-over. For the most professional finish, call a window cleaner with a good reputation in the area. For the next best thing at a fraction of the cost, do it yourself. Experts recommend you wash them twice a year at the very least, which doesn't sound unreasonable.

You'll need:

- One squeegee—the wide-headed tool with the smooth rubber blade which removes water without leaving dirty streaks. Available from all good DIY stores.
- A sponge—or for a more professional approach, a T-bar washer with a mop head. It's shaped like the letter 'T' and has a big mop on top. Also available from all good DIY stores.
- A bucket of cold water with a hearty dose of cleaning fluid—warm water is more likely to streak.

• A nice little chamois cloth.

Before you begin

Assess the weather: If it's sunny and the windows are hot, they'll dry too fast and streak, which you may have gathered by now is the worst thing that can happen in a window-cleaner's world (apart from falling off a ladder or through the pane). If it is warm and sunny, go and sit in the back garden and come back when it's cloudy, dry, and miserable.

Clean

It's a cloudy, dry, miserable day, so begin by removing any loose debris on or around the window. Use the mop head on the T-bar thing or your sponge and wash down the windowsills and frames. If you leave the sills and frames until after the window, you'll almost certainly splash water down your newly-cleaned, streak-free pane, and then you'll have to start again.

Wash

Soak your T-bar thing with just enough soapy water to cover the pane—you don't need to saturate it. Put your back into it to remove those stubborn stains, especially the grime you've allowed to build up in the corners of the frame. The professionals swear by a razor blade to scrape off any heavy-duty bird crap more easily, though the blade has to be wet or you'll scratch the glass.

Wipe

Before you squeegee the window, wet the blade with a damp cloth so that it doesn't 'skip' across the surface of the glass. Place the squeegee in the top left corner of the window, so the blade sits vertically and against the window edge.

Press it firmly and pull across the window in one sweeping movement. Wipe the squeegee dry with a paper towel (to avoid creating streaks), and then repeat on the section below, overlapping slightly so you cover the entire pane.

Pull, wipe clean, move down. Repeat the process until finally you reach the bottom, and wipe away any water at the base of the window frame with the damp chamois cloth—it soaks up water without leaving unsightly str—see if you can finish that sentence yourself, reader...

Falling down

There are many heroic and manly ways to meet your maker, but falling off a ladder with a squeegee in your hand is not one of them. If you need to reach just that little bit higher, buy a squeegee extender pole thing.

If you have to use a ladder, make sure it's angled safely (never more than 75 degrees), planted on stable ground, and that you never overreach, otherwise you'll be left hanging off the gutters or dead on the ground below. And nobody wants that. Or so you'd like to think...

A fine finish

According to people who wash their windows more often and thoroughly than you and I, a supreme finish can be achieved by scrunching up a sheet or two of old newspaper and polishing the now-clean glass. Others claim this'll leave you with ink down your nice clean windows.

Equally contentious is the suggestion that adding vinegar to your cleaning solution will guarantee a streak-free clean. Some say it works, others say it's bullshit.

How To...
Dance

To be more exact, that should read How To ... Dance Without Looking And Feeling Like A Club-Footed Asshole, or that tragic uncle who bounds around the floor at weddings looking like that guy from REM. Tragically, at some point in your life you'll be forced into a situation where you have to dance. When that happens, you'll either have to lock yourself in the bathroom or wish you'd paid closer attention to this page...

Some basic rules

1. Almost all men are shit dancers. Some know how to cover up their natural lack of rhythm better than you do, the rest don't care.

2. Most men who dance are making it up as they go along. They don't have an elaborate choreographed dance routine worked out. Watch them (on the sly) for more than six seconds and that much will become clear.

3. Most men who dance know that confidence goes a long way. Professional dancers refer to it as 'attitude': the ability to make others believe you know what you're doing.

4. Any man who has a basic move will elevate himself above the dance-floor shufflers. They will think you have natural rhythm, while you will know that you've simply followed The Most Basic Dance Move Ever Devised...

The most basic dance move ever devised...

Study any dance move closely enough and you'll find an element of the Step-Touch. So that's what you're learning today, and when you read how simple it is you'll be wondering if you can have your money back for this entry.

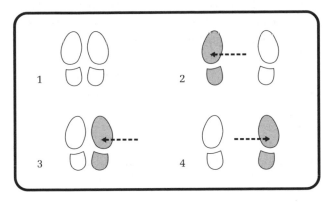

1. Stand with your legs a comfortable distance apart. No, only you can determine 'comfortable.'

2. Listen to the track and step one leg to the side *on the beat.*

3. Keeping on beat, bring the other leg over so that you're back in your starting position, albeit to the side of where you began.

4. On the next beat, repeat the move to the other side, and continue to repeat on alternative sides for the rest of the song.

5. There is no 5, that's really all there is to it.

The beauty of the Step-Touch is that the technique remains the same whether you go left or right, backwards or forwards. All you really need to remember is to step on the beat, otherwise you'll look foolish.

Now bring in the arms...

Bear in mind that if you're only moving your feet you're doing nothing more than a glorified shuffle. Introduce the arms and you progress to actual dancing. Arm action makes everything more expressive—which is where most men make asses of themselves.

The key is to keep both arms tight and project confidence, maybe even something approaching a jaunty swagger. Never let your arms hang down limply like you don't know what you're supposed to do with them—you now know that's not the point.

Start with the most basic arm move: a glorified jogging motion where they just appear to bounce up and down. You're right, it's kinda shitty, but it looks passable as long as you're still moving in time to the beat.

From there, build in something slightly more impressive. As you move your foot to the right, move your arms and point your right index finger that way, or roll your fists over each other in that direction. When you step onto the left foot, move your arms in the same direction.

Now, if you're confident enough with all that, you may as well pull out the classic 70s disco arm move. This time, as you step to the left, on the beat, push your left arm up high and point. Step back to the right and repeat on that side with your right arm and hand. Any dance is a statement, and your 70s disco move screams: 'I'm out of my depth, and I don't have any idea how to stop!'

So, that just about covers the most basic of basics. From here, both the legs and arms begin to move in ever more complex ways, and before you know it you're spinning on your head, which now sports an ill-advised afro. So yes, it's probably best we leave it at that for now.

How To...
Dance Properly, Like A Gentleman

For the more refined gentleman who considers himself above chasing loose women across sleazy dance floors using a crappy touch-step dance routine, it may be worth considering learning to dance like a gentleman.

Ballroom dancing has been around in various forms forever, give or take a few years. It used to be an upper-class pursuit, while the commoners were forced to content themselves with folk dancing and fighting bears. Nowadays, class doesn't count for much. Many of the more accomplished ballroom artists are loud-mouthed commoners soaked in fake tans and cheap jewelry.

If you were to ask them to recommend one dance move for the novice to learn, they'd probably suggest the Swing Boogie, Disco Fox, or Carolina Shag. But because we're looking to start with the basics and need to keep things simple, you might be better off mastering the basics of the waltz—a timeless classic taken from the German word *walzen*, meaning to glide. You're a man, so you should lead and she should follow. It turns out the basics are a cinch...

The Waltz

Face your partner and place your right hand on her waist, a little towards the back. Your left arm should be held out to the left, elbow bent and your palm raised about shoulder height to facing her. Her right hand should grasp your left loosely, her left hand should rest on your right shoulder, her elbow bent rather than fully outstretched. Now you're set, tell her to hang on, wait for the beat, and follow these steps.

Dance gracefully on the tips of your toes. Look straight ahead, which should be into her eyes or eye, if she's one of those women who wears a patch. The experts suggest you count 'one, two, three,' 'one, two, three' as you waltz, placing emphasis and moving off on the 'one' count.

On the first beat ('one'), step forward with your left foot, gliding as gracefully as possible. She should mirror your movement on each beat, so her right foot steps back.

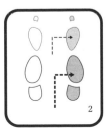

On the second beat ('two'), your right foot goes forwards and to the right, in the shape of an upside-down L. Your weight should be on the right foot, your left doesn't move.

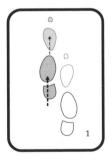

On the third beat ('three'), slide the left foot over to your right foot and stand with them together.

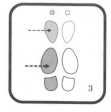

On the fourth ('one'), step the right foot back.

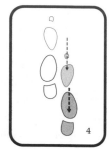

On the fifth ('two'), bring the left foot back and to the left, following the backwards and reversed L shape. At the end of this step your weight should be on the left foot.

On the final beat ('three'), slide the right foot back towards the left until they're side by side. You've completed stage one and are ready to step forward with the left foot again. Repeat the above until the music ends or you're out of breath, varying the placement of the feet slightly so you glide around the room a little instead of circling a small square plot of floor.

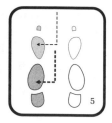

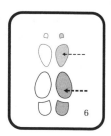

About the Author

Nick Harper is a tall journalist with a light beard. He has written for such esteemed publications as *The Guardian*, *FHM*, *FourFourTwo*, and *Men's Health*, alongside many other men who wouldn't know a jump lead from a giblet. This is his first go at books.

DAVID

JOYEUX NOËL

Rue Dieu

Nous donne

Longue

Vie